The Golden Rule &
the Games People Play

Other Books by Rami Shapiro

The Sacred Art of Lovingkindness: Preparing to Practice

Amazing Chesed: Living a Grace-Filled Judaism

Recovery—The Sacred Art: The Twelve Steps as Spiritual Practice

Writing—The Sacred Art: Beyond the Page to Spiritual Practice

In the SkyLight Illuminations Series

The Divine Feminine in Biblical Wisdom Literature:
Selections Annotated & Explained

Ecclesiastes: Annotated & Explained

Embracing the Divine Feminine: Finding God Through the Ecstasy of
Physical Love—The Song of Songs Annotated & Explained

Ethics of the Sages: Pirke Avot Annotated & Explained

Hasidic Tales: Annotated & Explained

The Hebrew Prophets: Selections Annotated & Explained

Perennial Wisdom for the Spiritually Independent:
Sacred Teachings—Annotated & Explained

Proverbs: Annotated & Explained

Tanya, the Masterpiece of Hasidic Wisdom:
Selections Annotated & Explained

The Golden Rule & the GAMES PEOPLE PLAY

The Ultimate Strategy for a Meaning-Filled Life

Rami Shapiro

Walking Together, Finding the Way®

SKYLIGHT PATHS®
PUBLISHING
Woodstock, Vermont

The Golden Rule and the Games People Play:
The Ultimate Strategy for a Meaning-Filled Life

2015 Quality Paperback Edition, First Printing
© 2015 by Rami Shapiro

All translations of sacred texts are the author's, unless otherwise noted.

Grateful acknowledgment is given for permission to use material from *The Essential Rumi*, by Jalal al-Din Rumi, translated by Coleman Barks (San Francisco: HarperSanFrancisco, 2004). Used with permission of Coleman Barks.

Library of Congress Cataloging-in-Publication Data
Shapiro, Rami M.
  The golden rule and the games people play : the ultimate strategy for a meaning-filled life / Rabbi Rami Shapiro.
    pages cm
  Includes bibliographical references.
   ISBN 978-1-59473-598-1 (pbk.) — ISBN 978-1-59473-606-3 (ebook)   1. Golden rule. 2. Ethics. 3. Game theory. I. Title.
  BL85.S385 2015
  177'.7—dc23
                                    2015027059

10 9 8 7 6 5 4 3 2 1

Manufactured in the United States of America
Cover and Interior Design: Tim Holtz
Cover Art: © Ralwel/Shutterstock

Walking Together, Finding the Way®
Published by SkyLight Paths Publishing
A Division of LongHill Partners, Inc.
Sunset Farm Offices, Route 4, P.O. Box 237
Woodstock, VT 05091
Tel: (802) 457-4000 Fax: (802) 457-4004
www.skylightpaths.com

To my dad, Archie Jack Shapiro, *z"l*,
who died during the writing of this book.
May his memory be a blessing to all who knew him.

Contents

Preface

This book goes against the conventional wisdom regarding the Golden Rule, but I think it adds a valuable voice to the conversation.

It rests on eight assumptions:

1. Life is a game.
2. There are two categories of games: finite zero-sum and infinite nonzero.
3. The goal of finite zero-sum games is to end the game with you as the winner.
4. In finite games, striving to be the winner requires at least indifference to others being losers.
5. The goal of infinite nonzero games is to keep the game going, and this means there are no ultimate winners or losers.
6. In infinite games, striving to maintain the game requires that you be sensitive and respond to the needs of others.
7. Life requires that we play both finite and infinite games, yet it is the infinite games that provide us with our greatest sense of meaning, joy, and purpose.
8. The Golden Rule is the best strategy for playing infinite games.

If you believe life isn't a game, there is no point in reading this book. Or if you believe that life is a finite game, a game of absolute winners and absolute losers, then put this book aside without reading it. If you deny that life is an infinite game, you will play the game to win, and to win absolutely, and the only way to win absolutely is to make sure others lose absolutely. This kind of play makes the Golden Rule the enemy of your deepest desire.

If you want to win, and winning is at the expense of others, "do to others as you would have them do to you" is a very poor strategy. If you want to play and to keep the game going for as long as you can and for as many people as you can, then the Golden Rule is the secret to playing wisely and well.

This is how I want to play. This is why I wrote this book. I hope this is why you will read it as well.

Introduction

The Golden Rule may be made of fool's gold: it looks like the most precious of ethical teachings, but in fact it proves false in most of our encounters with the world. Despite the fact that almost every religion touts it and almost everyone claims it as their ultimate moral guide, most of us do not follow it most of the time.

There are two possible reasons for this. First, we may be morally weak and ethically myopic and simply reject the Golden Rule as too high a bar for us to reach. Second, the Golden Rule may simply not apply in the vast number of interactions in which we engage. This book addresses the latter of the two.

The Golden Rule—"In everything do to others as you would have them do to you"—only works in the context of a certain kind of interaction, an interaction designed to maintain a relationship for as long as possible. I am calling such interactions infinite nonzero games, where the word "games" refers to any interaction in which we humans may engage.

The goal of an infinite nonzero game is to maintain the relationship between the "players," and the Golden Rule is indeed the best way to do this. But not all or even most of our exchanges are infinite nonzero games. Most of our exchanges are finite zero-sum games designed to produce winners and losers within a fixed time frame.

To make this plain, compare a friendship with a basketball game. The goal of a friendship is to maintain the friendship indefinitely, and one way to do that is to treat your friend as you would like to be treated by your friend. The goal of a basketball game is to defeat your opponent within the fixed time allotted by the rules of the game. Applying the Golden Rule in the context of basketball would eliminate the chances of anyone winning: after all, you wouldn't want someone to strip the basketball out of your grasp, so you would choose not to strip the ball out of an opponent's grasp.

This example may sound a bit silly, but the notion of examining the Golden Rule in the context of infinite nonzero and finite zero-sum games is not.

Take, for example, the 2015 uproar over the Religious Freedom Restoration Act (RFRA) passed, and then amended, in Indiana. Whatever its intent, the act seemed to allow for businesses to discriminate against customers if the customers' request of the business violated the faith of the owners of the business. The classic example is a caterer who refuses to cater a same-sex wedding because same-sex marriage violates her faith.

Whatever your opinion on RFRA or marriage equality, the Golden Rule would mandate that the caterer treat all her customers the way she would like to treated. Presumably she would not want to be discriminated against based on her sexual orientation, so she should, according to the Rule, not discriminate against her LGBTQ clientele. But in the mind of many, the Golden Rule just doesn't apply.

Or take the case of Ron Paul during the 2012 presidential primary. During a debate on American foreign policy, Congressman Paul said, "If another country does to us what we do to others, we're not going to like it very much. So I would say that maybe we ought to consider a 'Golden Rule' in foreign policy. Don't do to other nations what we don't want to have them do to us."

The crowd booed.

I suspect Congressman Paul was a bit shocked by his audience's response. After all, these were people largely if not overwhelmingly associated with the Christian faith in one form or another, and it is the founder of that faith who is most often, albeit incorrectly, credited with being the first to articulate the Golden Rule, that is, "In everything do to others as you would have them do to you" (Matthew 7:12). Jesus is more than a prophet or saint to most Christians; he is God incarnate. Here is God himself setting forth this rule, and here are God's people booing it!

What the audience in South Carolina revealed is this: When we want to love our neighbor, we cite the Golden Rule in support of doing so. When we want to bomb our neighbor, we ignore or even boo the Golden Rule and find some other divine command to justify our bombing.

What determines observance and nonobservance of an ethical rule, precept, or principle isn't the rule, precept, or principle itself but the situation in which you find yourself. If violence is perceived as necessary, violence will be condoned. If violence is perceived as unnecessary, violence will be condemned. Circumstances arising in specific times and places, not any universal principle, determine what we consider right or wrong.

In the case of Congressman Paul and the audience that booed the Golden Rule, we might assume—correctly, in my estimation—that they live in a profoundly zero-sum world. Theirs is a world of winners and losers and "us against them," where only one side can win. Because this is so, the Golden Rule is not only ignored but also actually derided.

Failure to live by the Golden Rule, therefore, has little or nothing to do with human frailty: "the spirit indeed is willing, but the flesh is weak" (Matthew 26:41) or Saint Paul's notion that "I do not understand my own actions. For I do not do what I want, but I do the very thing I hate" (Romans 7:15). Matthew is saying that we have conflicting drives, competing desires. It isn't that we want one thing or the other, but that we want one thing *and* the other. When we can have both, we grab both; when we can have but one, the stronger desire wins out. In other words, when the flesh defeats the spirit, it isn't because the flesh is weak but because it is stronger than the spirit. The weaker never wins.

Similarly with Saint Paul's notion that he does what he hates. Unless Paul suffers from a neurological disorder causing him to do what he hates against his will, his protestation about doing what he hates against his will is pure nonsense. While it may be true that we can prioritize our desires from the most desirable to the least, the one we choose to actualize isn't the one we hate but the one we prefer even as we deny the fact. If what we choose to do is hurtful or hateful, we might preface our actions by saying, "I hate to do this, but," yet what we are really saying is, "I know what I am doing is wrong, but I am doing it anyway because it is the one thing I want to do above all others."

Our choices are not made in a vacuum. They are driven by the circumstances in which we find ourselves, or rather our reading of those circumstances. This is troubling to anyone—myself included—who wants to find in the Golden Rule a universal guide to ethical behavior. If the Rule is so easily abandoned or manipulated, in what way is it a helpful guide at all?

Determining the Games and the Rule(s)

Rather than begin with the assumption that the Golden Rule is humanity's moral true north rooted in some extra-human or transcendent realm beyond human manipulation, we begin with the assumption that the Golden Rule is a rule only in certain circumstances. Given the right circumstance, the Golden Rule is not only the right choice but also the only choice.

Situations in which the applicability of the Golden Rule is questionable are called nonzero, and the exchanges between the participants in nonzero scenarios are called infinite games. Situations in which the Golden Rule does not apply are called zero-sum, and the participants in zero-sum scenarios are engaged in what we call finite games.

The aim of this book isn't to promote infinite games over finite ones. Nor am I insisting that the Golden Rule is universally golden or universally applicable. Rather, I am arguing that the most important games of life are infinite games—our relationships—and that within the context of these games the Golden Rule is golden and that it provides the ultimate strategy for playing well.

We all play both finite and infinite games, but it is the infinite games that provide us with the deeper sense of meaning and purpose that so many of us crave. Exploring the Golden Rule in the context of infinite games allows us to better understand and apply the Rule, to better understand and play infinite games, to better understand when we are playing a finite game when we ought to be playing an infinite one, and when we would be wise to shift from the rules of finite play to the Golden Rule of infinite play.

While playing finite games is natural and inevitable, playing only finite games is neither. In fact, living a joyous, loving, and meaning-filled life is directly linked to how much infinite play defines your life. Recognizing the need for infinite play opens up more and more opportunities for applying the Golden Rule, and the more we apply the Golden Rule, the more infinite our play becomes and the more opportunities for living the Golden Rule we have. This is a virtuous circle.

This book is not a standard survey of the Golden Rule in the world's religions or even a celebration of the Rule as the be-all and end-all of human ethical behavior. It is a series of reflections on the Golden Rule: how it works, why it works, and why it can and should be a guide to your daily interactions with beings human and otherwise.

I invite you to muse along with me.

The Games People Play

An Introduction to Game Theory

This book is about the Golden Rule—"In everything do to others as you would have them do to you"—and it only makes sense in a world of selves and others relating in ways that seek to maximize the benefit to both. The Golden Rule assumes we humans are social animals. After all, I cannot "do to others" if there are no others unto whom to do. As Aristotle wrote nearly twenty-four hundred years ago, "The individual, when isolated, is not self-sufficing; and therefore he is like a part in relation to the whole. But he who is unable to live in society, or who has no need because he is sufficient for himself, must be either a beast or a god."[1]

The individual is part of a whole and cannot survive separate from it. We depend on other humans and on nature to do for us what we cannot do for ourselves. For example, no matter how dependent I am on oxygen, and no matter how desperately my lungs may wish to produce oxygen if I am running out of it, the simple fact is they do not have the capacity to do so. The oxygen on which my very existence depends is produced by trees and plants in collaboration with earth, water, and sun. While I am very proficient at producing other gases, I am totally incapable of producing the one gas I need the most. I am dependent on nature for my survival, and I am a part of the interdependent web of natural interactions—interactions I am calling "games."

The same is true regarding my dependency on other human beings. While it is possible that I could, given sufficient time and training, learn to grow all my own food, fix all my own appliances, and make my own clothes, the probability of my doing so is remote. And when it comes to more complicated devices such as my computer and car, and resources such as the gas that fuels my car and the natural gas that heats and cools my house, I would have to learn to do without rather than secure these by myself.

My lifestyle depends on the global village, just as my life depends on the global biosphere. I am not what Aristotle calls "a beast or a god," and I am—happily, as it turns out—a part in relation to a whole. I suspect what is true of me is true of you as well.

The Game of Life

"Game" is the name I am giving to our interactions with one another and with all life. I'm borrowing the term from two sources. The less formal source is Milton Bradley's *The Game of Life*. Created in 1860, it was originally called the *Checkered Game of Life*, "checkered" referring to the board on which the game was played rather than to any thoughts on life Mr. Bradley may have held. With its introduction in the mid-nineteenth century, the phrase "game of life" entered the zeitgeist. As the American artist and New Thought spiritual teacher Florence Scovel Shinn (1871–1940) wrote:

> Most people consider life a battle, but it is not a battle, it is a game. It is a game, however, which cannot be played successfully without the knowledge of spiritual law, and the Old and New Testaments give the rules of the game with wonderful clearness. Jesus Christ taught that it was a great game of Giving and Receiving.[2]

Shinn's reference to giving and receiving may have been an oblique reference to the Golden Rule as Jesus articulated it: "In everything do to others as you would have them do to you." While, as we shall see, I take issue with the notion that reciprocity is at the heart of the Golden Rule, if it is the Rule that Shinn is referencing, then I agree: it is at the heart of what it means to play the game of life well.

The more formal source of my use of "game" is game theory, the study of strategic decision making. Game theory is most often applied in the fields of economics, psychology, and political science, though here we apply it to ethics in general and the Golden Rule in particular.

In game theory, there are two fundamental categories of games: finite zero-sum games and infinite nonzero games. Finite zero-sum games, as the word "finite" makes clear, come to an end when one person or team wins and the other person or team loses. The sole purpose of a finite game is to win, and winning is always achieved at the expense of the other losing.

Baseball, for example, is a finite zero-sum game played out over nine innings. Most games end when one team has scored more runs than the other within the innings allowed. In the event of a tie, more innings are played until one team defeats the other.

Things are very different with infinite nonzero games. The goal of an infinite nonzero game is—as the word "infinite" suggests—to keep the game going. As long as the game is maintained, everyone wins, though not necessarily equally. It is because an infinite game is non-zero that participants have a vested interest in keeping the game going. Losing in the context of an infinite game means that the game comes to an end and becomes a finite game, and when it does, everyone loses, though, again, not necessarily equally.

A loving friendship is a good example of an infinite nonzero game. The goal of friendship is to keep the friendship going. Unlike in finite games, the goal isn't for one friend to win something at the expense of the other friend. Winning at the expense of one's friend would risk bringing the friendship to an end, something neither friend desires.

Given this dynamic, players of infinite nonzero games continually adjust the rules to keep the game in play. Where players of finite zero-sum games insist that the rules of the game are permanent and followed to the letter, players of infinite nonzero games change the rules whenever necessary to keep the game going. Where finite gamers play within the rules of the game, infinite gamers make playing with the rules part of the game.

For example, imagine you are pitching in a softball game. Imagine as well that you are someone who tries to live by the Golden Rule: doing to others as you would have them do to you. Knowing that if you were the batter you would want the pitcher to pitch in a way that would maximize your ability to hit the ball, you choose to pitch in a way that leads to the batter's success.

If the batter were following the same ethic, knowing that you would want her to strike out rather than hit the ball, she chooses to swing and miss regardless of how hittable your pitch might be.

Put simply, if softball were played by the Golden Rule, the game would end quickly with no hits or runs. But, of course, that isn't how the game is played. Why? Because softball is not an infinite nonzero game but a finite zero-sum game. The Golden Rule simply makes no sense in this setting.

Now apply the Golden Rule to a relationship between you and a close friend. Imagine you and your friend are having a heated argument, perhaps over the applicability of the Golden Rule to softball. At first you may hope to win the argument, and you can surmise that your friend wants to win as well. This sounds like a zero-sum competition, but it dawns on you that the argument could actually bring the game—the friendship itself—to an end. So you begin to soften your position and find ways of agreeing with parts of your friend's position. I'm not saying that either of you abandon your respective positions altogether, only that you both realize that maintaining the friendship trumps winning the argument.

Applying the Golden Rule in this scenario, you will find a way of saving face for both of you as a way of saving the relationship. Assuming you both desire to maintain the game, you will both take the Golden Rule as your guide and find a way to end the argument without ending the relationship. In all likelihood this will result in some level of compromise and the abandonment not of one's convictions but of one's need to win.

The Golden Rule makes no sense when playing finite zero-sum games. The Golden Rule makes consummate sense when playing infinite nonzero games. The reason the Golden Rule is so rarely followed is not because we are weak or wicked, but because the games we most often play don't call for it.

The Prisoner's Dilemma

Since game theory is so central to our discussion of the Golden Rule, it will be valuable to us to apply the Golden Rule to one of the classic games explored by game theorists. The Prisoner's Dilemma can take many different narrative forms. Here we will use a simple one explored in Laszlo Mero's book *Moral Calculations: Game Theory, Logic, and Human Frailty*.[3]

You and an accomplice, a person to whom you have no ties and for whom you have no feelings, have committed a serious crime but have done so cleverly enough that there is no usable evidence that can convict either of you in a court of law. The police and prosecuting attorney know the two of you are guilty but cannot prove it.

Shortly after the crime, you and your accomplice are arrested for driving under the influence (DUI). This charge the prosecutor can make stick. Upon your arrest, you and your partner are placed in separate cells. The prosecutor speaks to each of you privately and offers you each a plea bargain. If you confess to the larger serious crime and blame it on your partner, the prosecutor will set you free and focus her energies on convicting and imprisoning your partner for ten years. The catch is that you must confess while your partner does not confess. If you both confess, you will both be charged with the crime, and you will each go to prison for five years.

Of course, the prosecutor explains, if neither of you confesses, neither of you can be convicted of the crime—the evidence necessary to do so is lacking—and both of you will be charged with a DUI and will each spend one year in prison on account of it.

What will you do?

Remember, you feel no allegiance to your accomplice, and your sole aim is to get free as quickly as possible. If you confess and your accomplice does not, you are freed immediately. If you confess and your accomplice also confesses, you will be jailed for five years. If you don't confess but your accomplice does confess, you will be jailed for ten years. If you both refuse to confess, you will be jailed for one year.

There are two ways to play this game: zero-sum or nonzero sum. If you choose to engage from the perspective of zero-sum, you act in your own best interest without consideration of the other, assuming that the other is doing the same. In this case, there are only two options: confess first or not at all. In a zero-sum game, these two options are not equal. Assuming your accomplice will do what is in his best interest, and assuming that means avoiding jail time altogether by confessing first and blaming you, that is the strategy you will choose. There has to be a winner and there has to be a loser, and so you opt to win, defining winning as no jail time rather than less or equal jail time.

Now let's apply the Golden Rule to the Prisoner's Dilemma. How does "do to others as you would have them do to you" lead you to play the game?

The goal is the same: serve as little jail time as possible. Without the Golden Rule, you and your accomplice are in a zero-sum game, and your best bet is to confess first. Add the Golden Rule to the equation, however, and things change, because your concern is no longer zero-sum—your own fate—but nonzero, the fate of your accomplice as well.

What you want is to serve little or no jail time. Following the Golden Rule, you want the same for your accomplice. If you confess first and your accomplice doesn't confess, you win and he loses, which by the standards of the Golden Rule means you lose as well. If you both confess, the amount of time you spend in prison is less but not the least available to you. In this case, again following the values of the Golden Rule, you both lose even though your losses are equitable.

Following the Golden Rule, the only option available to you is to remain silent. In this way, if your accomplice does the same, you will each serve one year, which, given the Golden Rule, is the best possible outcome. But what are the chances your accomplice will do the same?

Your answer to this question will determine whether or not you follow the Golden Rule. If you assume your accomplice will not follow the

Rule and that the game being played is zero-sum, chances are you will do to your accomplice as you imagine your accomplice is about to do to you. Not exactly the Golden Rule at all. In fact, it's the opposite rule: an eye for an eye. But if, on the other hand, you assume your accomplice will follow the Rule and keep silent, your only option is to keep silent as well.

Is the Golden Rule Logical?

Is the application of the Golden Rule the outcome of logical analysis or simply the only rational strategy if you live life from the nonzero perspective? I suggest logic is not part of the Golden Rule, but that the Rule is the only option open to you when playing infinite nonzero games. Laszlo Mero, a mathematician and author of *Moral Calculations: Game Theory, Logic, and Human Frailty*, goes even further:

> The golden rule is not a rule of logic. It is not a *form of logical reasoning*, but rather it determines the *logic of value selection*, something that does not usually fall under the purview of traditional logic. Traditional logic, that is, the study of correct forms of reasoning, is here being supplemented by an additional, ethical, principle. This principle does not contradict traditional logic but neither does it follow from it. Logic applies with equal force to a world where the golden rule prevails as to one in which it does not. In the latter world, logic concludes that cooperating is not worthwhile. In the former, logic concludes that prisoner's dilemmas do not exist.[4]

But, of course, scenarios such as the Prisoner's Dilemma do exist. So does the Golden Rule matter or not? The answer depends on the game we are playing. The Golden Rule is *the* guide for infinite nonzero games but not for finite zero-sum ones.

The assumption at the foundation of this entire book is that the Golden Rule makes sense only in an infinite nonzero game worldview. If winning at the expense of others is the necessary consequence of living, if Aristotle is wrong and life is in fact a finite zero-sum game of you against all, then the Golden Rule is rarely if ever a wise strategy. If, on the other hand, winning is possible only when there are no losers, that is, if Aristotle is correct and life is an infinite nonzero game where each person plays her part for the benefit of all the other parts and hence the whole, then the Golden Rule is the rule to follow in almost every case.

Categorical Imperative

I hedge my bets with the word "almost" because, given the enormity of life situations, I cannot pretend to know what is best in every case. This is the exact opposite of Immanuel Kant's *categorical imperative.* In his book *Foundations of the Metaphysics of Morals,* Kant (1724–1804) explains that a categorical imperative is an unconditional, self-evident, and purely rational ethical maxim that must be acted upon regardless of the situation. For Kant the categorical imperative is the basis for the Golden Rule.

While Kant argues for the rationality of the categorical imperative, he does so based on a nonrational, though by no means irrational, assumption: that you will care about another person as you care about yourself.[5] That is to say, you will see the other as an end in herself and not as a means to your own ends. This is simply another way of saying that the Golden Rule and the categorical imperative arise from a world-view of infinite nonzero games.

The Golden Rule is a categorical imperative if and only if one's worldview is nonzero. The Rule is a strategy for playing an infinite game and not an a priori truth in and of itself. Everything depends on your worldview.

Warning

The Golden Rule May Be Hazardous to Your Faith

It is commonplace to celebrate the fact that almost every religion articulates the Golden Rule in one form or another, and the ubiquitous nature of the Rule is often heralded as the key to bridging the gap between religions and eradicating conflict among them. If each religion would emphasize its version of the Golden Rule, we are told, and if each would make the Golden Rule the heart of its teaching, all competition and conflict among the world's religions would end. Since every religion teaches its followers to treat others as they themselves want to be treated, Golden Rule–centered religions would cease to demonize one another, would abandon all efforts to convert members of another faith to its set of beliefs, and would eschew murdering of both those who choose not to convert to their faith and those who choose to convert out of their faith and into another.

What is not mentioned is that the Golden Rule itself is never the heart of a religion or even the focus of a religion. Indeed, you cannot build a religion around the Golden Rule because the Rule places all the power in the hands of the individual, while religion locks it firmly in the hands of the clergy or some other leadership class.

Religion versus the Rule

Although it is difficult to come up with a definition of "religion" that everyone can accept or that fits every example of religion worldwide, one trait that almost every religion seems to exhibit is that of institutional hierarchy. There is always a priestly caste, scholar class, or some other elite cadre of leaders, historically men, that determines what is true, sacred, revelatory, and obligatory regarding the religion they dominate. And these leaders rarely if ever focus on the Golden Rule.

It is not difficult to see why this is so. The problem that the Golden Rule solves—how to create and maintain infinite nonzero interactions with other beings—has nothing to do with the problems religions and religious leaders face:

- Defining what their religion stands for, and who is in and who is out of their religion
- What their religion upholds and what it condemns: what is the true creed or correct belief and what is heresy
- What constitutes legitimate ritual and practice and what violates it
- What the religion promises those who adhere to it in this life or a next life, and what it threatens will happen to those who reject its beliefs and the authority of those who establish and police those beliefs
- What is sexual purity, who is allowed to marry whom, and so forth

Furthermore, the Golden Rule requires no sacred text, no organized clergy, and no creed. It transcends any notion of ethnicity, race, tribe, nationality, or any other way we humans invent to separate ourselves from each other. The Golden Rule doesn't belong to any one religion, nor does it carry any exclusive religious brand. There is no Jewish Golden Rule in opposition to a Buddhist Golden Rule. There is simply the Golden Rule articulated in slightly different ways at different times and in different settings, but always making the same point: treating others as you want them to treat you.

The Golden Rule, unlike religion—even those religions that herald the Golden Rule—is self-evident in the sense that what I like and do not like are the measures of my actions. I don't need a god or messenger of god to explain these to me. Indeed, with the exception of the Rule as articulated by Jesus, whom most Christians take to be divine, the Golden Rule in the other world's religions is taught by quite ordinary humans: Confucius, Hillel, Buddha, and Muhammad, to name but four. Although the followers of these sages created vast hierarchical systems out of their teachings, they did not do so based on the Golden Rule.

In a speech delivered in San Francisco on April 8, 1900, Swami Vivekananda, one of the greatest teachers of Indian philosophy and founder of the Ramakrishna Order of Vedanta Hinduism, argued that for a religion to be successful it needs three things: a sacred text, a charismatic leader or founder who becomes the ideal toward which one strives, and a sense of exclusivity—the notion that it alone is true.[1] The Golden Rule lacks all three elements. Greater still, it renders all three of them moot.

Although it appears in many texts held sacred by one group or another, the Golden Rule itself doesn't rely on textual revelation at all, but only on self-observation. Although it is true that a revered leader may teach the Golden Rule, it isn't the teacher who gives it value but rather the self-evident nature of the teaching itself. Since the Golden Rule is global, there can be no sense of exclusivity or ownership by any one religion. Add to this the fact that you cannot, and more importantly need not, build an institution around the Rule or a political or priestly hierarchy upon it. The Golden Rule, for all its wisdom, just doesn't have what it takes to be the central tenant of any faith.

A Measure of Quality

On the contrary, as the great historian of religion Karen Armstrong argues, the Golden Rule is the measure by which we test the quality of our beliefs and not the product of any belief system in particular:

> The test is simple: if people's beliefs—secular or religious—make them belligerent, intolerant, and unkind about other people's faith, they are not "skillful." If, however, their convictions impel them to act compassionately and to honor the stranger, then they are good, helpful, and sound. This is the test of true religiosity in every single one of the major traditions.[2]

In Armstrong's estimation, the quality of a religion should be judged by its capacity to adhere to the Golden Rule. In her 2012 Charter for Compassion, Armstrong asserts that "the principle of compassion lies at the heart of all religious, ethical, and spiritual traditions, calling us always to treat all others as we wish to be treated ourselves."[3]

Although I would take issue with the claim that compassion is at the heart of all religions, I applaud and participate in the efforts of the Charter for Compassion movement. The reason why the world's religions have yet to support this effort and be transformed in its light is not hard to find. The Charter for Compassion goes on to say that "compassion can break down political, dogmatic, ideological, and religious boundaries."[4]

I agree, and the fact that compassion and the Golden Rule can do so is the very reason why religious leaders resist transforming their respective religions into vehicles for global compassion.

Organized religions are all about establishing and maintaining boundaries—political, dogmatic, ideological, and religious. The Golden Rule erases these or at the very least challenges their hegemony and by extension the power and authority claimed by those who declare and defend these boundaries.

Although I agree that we should use compassion, especially as it is articulated in the Golden Rule, as a gauge to judge the quality and spiritual authenticity of every faith, I doubt that any faith officially does so or will do so on its own. I suggest we use the Golden Rule as an independent measure of religion rather than imagine that religions can critique themselves by this metric.

Religion: Playing to Win

Not too long ago I was asked to join with several local ministers and our local imam to draft a brief statement decrying all violence done in the name of God. It took us but moments to affirm the Golden Rule and to write a statement rooted in it: "We the undersigned categorically reject all violence done in the name of God and religion." Each of us cited the Golden Rule as our guide when it came to writing, signing, and publishing this statement.

This was so easy to do that I took the opportunity of our meeting to encourage my colleagues to amend the statement with six additional words: "We the undersigned categorically reject all violence done in the name of God and religion *in this world and the next.*" The reaction was swift and negative.

Although each of us was willing to apply the Golden Rule in this life, when it came to applying it in our imagined afterlife scenarios I was an outlier. "This is God's business," I was told. "We cannot dictate to God what God will do with a soul after its time on earth has ended."

In other words, it's one thing to say that we shouldn't treat one another harshly over our differences in belief in this world, but if God wants to condemn nonbelievers to eternal damnation in the afterlife, that is God's business and we have nothing to say about it.

Arguing as I did that our ideas about God and what God can and will do are just that—our ideas—and that none of us knows anything about God beyond the all-too-human propositions promoted by our respective religions got me nowhere, and these six words never appeared in the published statement.

What was clear to me was that as Americans we lacked the power to inflict this-worldly harm on those whose beliefs place them outside our chosen boundaries, but as believers in what are essentially finite zero-sum religions, we still fantasize about doing so in the next life. Indeed, these fantasies are how we maintain the very boundaries the Golden Rule tears down.

While I'm willing to accept the claim that Confucius, Buddha, Hillel, Jesus, and Muhammad each held up the Golden Rule as the heart of his personal teaching, the religions and systems of practice and belief that arose from those teachings did not, and for the foreseeable future will not.

The reason for this has nothing to do with the intent of the founders and everything to do with the nature of finite and infinite games and zero-sum and nonzero thinking. The Golden Rule is the ultimate rule when playing infinite nonzero games: games that seek to break down barriers and boundaries, and indefinitely perpetuate relationships between all beings, and that do so by making the concerns of the other equal to our own.

This is not the game religion plays. Religion is rarely infinite or nonzero and is most often finite and zero-sum. Religions differ in profound ways—ways that are important to each faith and that determine the fate of their respective believers in this life and the next. While it is commonplace to hear people claim that all religions teach the same thing, this is patently false.

Christianity, for example, is nothing without the belief that Jesus is the Son of God and for most Christians the singular source of salvation. Yet the other religions of the world reject this claim categorically. At the heart of Buddhism isn't the Golden Rule, but the teaching of suffering and the ending of suffering. Although rooting your behavior in the Golden Rule may help alleviate suffering on some level, only the Eightfold Path of Buddhist thought and practice can do so completely, a claim that the other religions of the world reject.

It isn't tangential to Hinduism that there are many gods or the one Brahman, nor is the denial of gods tangential to Buddhism. The notion that the Hebrew Bible is the one true revelation from God is central to Judaism and cannot be set aside out of respect to the Muslim claim that only the Holy Qur'an can make this claim.

Religions are playing finite zero-sum games: they want to win in this life and the next, and they promise their followers that they will win, if not in this life then in the next, as long as those followers are loyal to whatever teachings, texts, and leadership the religion upholds. For one religion to win, the others must lose. Figuring out who wins and how one wins and what happens to those who lose is at the heart of religion and the central task of those who lead these religions. The Golden Rule has nothing to do with any of this.

Exposing the Fantasy

I realize that talking this way is upsetting to many, especially those who want to avoid religious conflict by taking refuge in a fantasy of religious unity. My mentor Huston Smith, one of the great scholars of the world's religions, uses the metaphor of mountain climbing to suggest that all religions are the same:

> It is possible to climb life's mountain from any side, but when the top is reached the trails converge. At base, in the foothills of theology, ritual, and organizational structure, the religions are distinct.... But beyond these differences, the same goal beckons.[5]

The implication is that the goal all religions share is universal peace, love, and acceptance, but this isn't the case at all. The goal that beckons is winning, and each religion defines what it is to win and how one goes about winning in different ways.

If the goal at the summit were the Golden Rule or universal compassion, there would be no need to climb the mountain at all. Each religion would simply encourage people to adhere to the Rule from the foothills on. Indeed, we would have no need for religion at all, which is really what adherents to this "all religions are the same" philosophy imply: "The fundamentals or essentials of all religions are the same. There is difference only in the non-essentials."[6]

Why bother with nonessentials? Why cling to beliefs that are unique to your religion if uniqueness itself reveals these beliefs to be nonessential? If we would only hold to the essential, religious differences would be irrelevant, and the religions that cling to these differences would disappear. But they don't because we can't because they aren't. Only those outside a given faith tradition can call the things that make that tradition unique nonessential. Only those who are willing not to scale the mountain to its summit, but to step off the path at the foothills and embrace the Golden Rule rather than the nonessential rules of religion, can afford to ignore what billions of believers live for, die for, and all too often kill to protect.

My claim isn't that all religions converge at the mountaintop of the Golden Rule, but that the Golden Rule invites us to climb a different mountain altogether. My claim isn't that all religions are variations of the Golden Rule, but that the Golden Rule is often at odds with religion, even those that claim it as their own.

Testing this claim will be the focus of the next two chapters of this book, but before we begin let's take a moment to distinguish between the two primary articulations of the Rule—one positive, the other negative—to see whether they matter.

Do Unto or Do Not Unto: That Is the Question

The most famous articulation of the Golden Rule in the West comes from Jesus and is couched in the positive: "In everything do to others as you would have them do to you" (Matthew 7:12, NRSV; Luke 6:31). But the earliest articulation of the Golden Rule comes from Confucius and is couched in the negative: "What you do not wish done to yourself do not do to others" (*Analects* 15:24). Does it matter which you follow?

According to ethicist Peter Singer:

> Prohibitions are generally easier to comply with than broad positive injunctions, and this must be part of the explanation for the greater number of rules beginning "Do not ..." rather than "Do ...." Compare "Do not kill innocent human beings" with "Preserve innocent human lives." The latter seems the better rule, for fewer innocent people will die if everyone tries to prevent their deaths than if everyone merely refrains from killing, allowing illnesses, accidents, and famines to take their full toll. The problem is that whereas "Do not kill innocent human beings" is compatible with a normal, relaxed way of life, "Preserve innocent human lives" could—in a time of

famine, for instance—require us to give up everything and work full-time to save the lives of others.[7]

In other words, the negative command is more likely to elicit compliance than is the positive command. Whether or not you agree with Dr. Singer, in the context of this book I leave the question of why one civilization opts for the negative articulation while another prefers the positive to cultural anthropologists. Instead, I consider both versions of the rule as ethically equivalent, since each is rooted in the notion of infinite nonzero games.

With this in mind, let's take a look at a sampling of the world's religions and how they deal with the Golden Rule. My goal isn't to provide an encyclopedic look at the Golden Rule in all the world's religions, but merely to take examples of the Golden Rule in some of these religions as paradigmatic of the Rule and religion in general. For convenience sake, we begin with so-called Eastern religions: Hinduism, Buddhism, and Confucianism (Hinduism being the oldest of the world's religions, and Confucianism being the first to articulate the Golden Rule as we know it today). In the following chapter we take up three of the Abrahamic faiths: Judaism, Christianity, and Islam.

Again, this list of six faiths is not inclusive, and much can be said about the Golden Rule in faiths such as Sikhism, Baha'i, and the earth-honoring religions. If this were an encyclopedia of the Golden Rule, exploring these and other religions would be *de rigeur*, but it is not. Our goal isn't to prove that the Golden Rule finds its way into every religion but to see why it is not at the heart of any of them.

Evading the Rule in Hinduism, Buddhism, and Confucianism

Many who see themselves as spiritually liberal and open to interfaith encounters believe that the Golden Rule lies at the heart of every religion. The truth is otherwise. While every religion has a version of the Golden Rule, no religion makes the Rule its ethical benchmark. It isn't that religions are imperfect, but that the Golden Rule and the infinite nonzero game it requires is antithetical to the finite zero-sum games religions play. In and of itself the Golden Rule doesn't shatter the limitations of the cultures in which it arises. It is an infinite nonzero outlier in a game that is overwhelmingly finite and zero-sum.

In this and the following chapter I will highlight how religions both articulate and then ignore the Golden Rule. My point is not to denigrate these religions or cultures, but simply to note that the Golden Rule when articulated in a particular religion is not an independent standard of ethical behavior.

Hinduism

Hinduism, like all religions, plays two games: an infinite nonzero game rooted in universal justice and compassion, and a finite zero-sum game rooted in ancient tribal cultures. When these two games come into conflict, it is most often the latter that wins. In the context of Hinduism this is more obvious in the zero-sum game of caste and patriarchy.

Hindus rarely speak of Hinduism, and when they do it is in compliance with European religious classifications rather than any self-understanding on the part of the Indian people themselves. The word *Hindu* is Persian and was adapted from the Sanskrit word *Sindhu*, referring to the Indus River. Muslims in the eighth century CE used *Hindu* to refer to the millions of people living in and beyond the Indus valley. Europeans adopted the term and in the late 1700s began to use it to refer to all followers of Indian religions, and some decades later they introduced the term "Hinduism" to refer to the entire spectrum of religions indigenous to India, as if all Indian religions could be seen as variations of a core set of beliefs.

Given the imposition of the term "Hinduism" on a variety of distinct faiths, it isn't surprising that Hinduism seems to have no single founder, text, principle, practice, or goal. How could it? To expect otherwise would be the equivalent of lumping Judaism, Christianity, Islam, and Baha'i into a single religion called, let's say, Abrahamism and then expecting them to share a single sacred literature, practice, and goal. They don't. They are separate religions. This is no less true of the many faiths found in the Indian subcontinent.

Yet the Indian peoples do share a common folk literature found in two massive collections of stories called the Ramayana and the Mahabharata. Both collections are called *itihāsa*, historical narratives containing teachings that define the proper aims of human life and how to achieve them. The Ramayana is the older of the two books and, in its current form, contains over fifty thousand verses. While the Ramayana is said to be the work of a single author, the poet-sage Valmiki, it has gone through numerous revisions by various authors over the centuries. The oldest extant manuscript of the Ramayana, an eleventh-century copy written on palm leaves, was found in Nepal.

Valmiki's Ramayana, written some time between the fourth and fifth centuries BCE, is the tale of Prince Rama, whose wife Sita is kidnapped by the demon-king Ravana. The title Ramayana is best translated as "Rama's Journey," referring to Rama's adventures to free his wife and bring her home.

The Mahabharata is attributed to the sage Vyasa and was composed shortly after the Ramayana. The plot of the Mahabharata centers around the Kurukshetra War, a civil war between two clans of cousins, the Kaurava and the Pandava. The most famous story within the Mahabharata is the Bhagavad Gita, the Song (*Gita*) of God (*Bhagavan*). In this tale, Prince Arjuna of the Pandava is about to lead his warriors in what will be the bloody destruction of their Kaurava cousins. The thought of slaughtering family is anathema to Arjuna, and the prince turns to his charioteer for advice. The latter turns out to be Lord Krishna, the Supreme God incarnate in human form, and through a series of dialogues Krishna articulates to Arjuna the key teachings of the Upanishads, the Indian philosophical literature.

Like their Greek equivalents, Homer's *Iliad* and *Odyssey*, the Ramayana and Mahabharata were not read as mere story. They contain the adventures of the ancient Gods and use narrative form to impart deep spiritual and philosophical ideas and teachings.

It is in the Mahabharata that we find the earliest expressions of the Indian version of the Golden Rule: "Don't do unto others that, which if done to you, would cause you suffering; this is the sum of all *dharma* [duty]" (Mahabharata 5.1517).

The philosophical foundation of this teaching is given in the Manusmrti, or Laws of Manu, an encyclopedia of Indian moral teachings and ethical behavior given to Manu by Brahma, the Creator God, and compiled sometime between 200 BCE and 200 CE:

> One who sees Me in all beings,
> and all beings in Me,
> And who serves Me by serving all beings;
> Such a one alone acts rightly
> and realizes the Highest Self.
> One who sees the wives of others as his mother,
> And who sees another's gold as if it were dross,
> And whose compassion for others
> equals compassion for self,
> This one alone is truly wise.[1]

What Manu has laid out here is the key teaching central to all infinite nonzero relationships and hence to the Golden Rule, which is the guide to correctly engaging in such relationships. Yet in the Manavadharma-sastra, another collection of laws attributed to Manu and dating from the time of the Mahabharata, we are told the following:

> A girl, a young woman, or even an old woman should not do anything independently, even in her own house. In childhood a woman should be under her father's control, in youth under her husband's, and when her husband is dead, under her sons'. She should not have independence.[2]

This notion of a woman's dependence is reinforced in the section dealing with marriage:

> I will tell the eternal duties of a man and wife who stay on the path of duty both in union and separation. Men must make their women dependent day and night, and keep under their own control those who are attached to sensory objects. Her father guards her in childhood, her husband guards her in youth, and her sons guard her in old age. A woman is not fit for independence.[3]

If independence is a value for some, and the Golden Rule is a guide to all, why isn't independence a value for women as well as men? While it is anachronistic to compare the ethical standards of ancient India to those of modern India or the West in general, it is not anachronistic to note that when doing unto women in that society, one would never imagine that what a woman would want would be to be independent. Independence for women would have been unthinkable at the time these texts were written, and no moral standard would have or even could have challenged their status.

So here we see that having the Golden Rule expressed in a religion is not sufficient to shape that religion in the Rule's image. The system in which the Rule operates, the game the people are playing, matters far more. The Indian system of caste makes this all the more clear.

There are four primary castes in classical India: Brahman, Kshatriya, Vaishya, and Shudra: Priests, Rulers, Merchants, and Laborers. A fifth category of persons, the untouchables, was thought to be so vile that any contact with them was polluting. Your caste is determined by your birth, and your birth is determined by your karma—the quality of life you lived prior to your current birth. Quality of life here is determined not by a universal system of ethical behavior, but by living strictly in accordance with the rules of the caste into which you are born. You move up the caste system in subsequent births by adhering strictly to the code of conduct assigned to the caste of your present birth.

> Society works best if each group follows its proper function.... Which caste one is born into depends on how one lived in a previous life; a good life moves you up, while a bad life moves you down. So those of lower caste are getting what they deserve, being punished for sins of a previous life. The caste system remains influential, even though India outlawed it in 1948.[4]

The caste system is a finite zero-sum game of winners and losers. In that system, the Golden Rule can apply only within a caste and not between castes. And the limitation of the Rule is reinforced by the metaphysical notion of karma: things are as they are because things were as they were; you are what you are because you were what you were. Justice is absolute, but only in the finite zero-sum context.

Buddhism

When many of us think of Buddhism we think of His Holiness the Fourteenth Dalai Lama, Thich Nhat Hanh, Pema Chödrön, and Ajahn Chah, each of whom espouses an infinite nonzero Buddhism rooted in nonviolence and compassion, and certainly in sync with the Golden Rule. Yet Buddhists, no less than the rest of us, are easily trapped in a finite zero-sum tribalism that excuses and even applauds actions that violate the Golden Rule.

Although resting on the foundational teachings of Siddhartha Gautama (563–483 BCE), the Indian seeker of the Kshatriya caste who came to be called Buddha, the Awakened One, Buddhism is not interested in union with or worship of a god or gods, however defined, but rather with the liberation of people from suffering (*dukkha*). At the heart of Buddhism are two sets of teachings attributed to the Buddha himself: the Four Noble Truths and the Noble Eightfold Path.

The Four Noble Truths speak to the nature of samsara, the endless cycle of birthing, dying, and rebirthing that is the world you and I experience. What drives samsara is ignorance (*avidya*) of how best to live one's life. It is because of our ignorance that we live with *trishna* (Sakskrit; *tanha*, Pali), endless craving after goals that cannot be achieved (Second Noble Truth). Because these goals are unachievable, we experience life as *dukkha*, suffering (First Noble Truth). *Dukkha* is overcome by ending *trishna*, and *trishna* ceases when we move from ignorance to knowledge and attain Nirvana, cessation of craving (Third Noble Truth). The way to make this shift is called the Noble Eightfold Path (Fourth Noble Truth).

> In the same way I saw an ancient path, an ancient road, traveled by the Rightly Self-awakened Ones of former times. And what is that ancient path, that ancient road, traveled by the Rightly Self-awakened Ones of former times? Just this noble eightfold path: right view, right aspiration, right speech, right action, right livelihood, right effort, right mindfulness, right concentration.... I followed that path. Following it, I came to direct knowledge of aging & death, direct knowledge of the origination of aging & death, direct knowledge of the cessation of aging & death, direct knowledge of the path leading to the cessation of aging & death.... Knowing that directly, I have revealed it to monks, nuns, male lay followers & female lay followers. (*Nagara Sutta*)[5]

At the heart of Right View, the first element of the Noble Eightfold Path, is the notion of *pratitya samutpada*, interdependent co-arising. The Vietnamese Zen Master Thich Nhat Hanh explains the idea this way:

Pratitya samutpada is sometimes called the teaching of cause and effect, but that can be misleading, because we usually think of cause and effect as separate entities, with cause always preceding effect, and one cause leading to one effect. According to the teaching of Interdependent Co-Arising, cause and effect co-arise (*samutpada*) and everything is a result of multiple causes and conditions.... In the sutras, this image is given: "Three cut reeds can stand only by leaning on one another. If you take one away, the other two will fall." For a table to exist, we need wood, a carpenter, time, skillfulness, and many other causes. And each of these causes needs other causes to be. The wood needs the forest, the sunshine, the rain, and so on. The carpenter needs his parents, breakfast, fresh air, and so on. And each of those things, in turn, has to be brought about by other causes and conditions. If we continue to look in this way, we'll see that nothing has been left out. Everything in the cosmos has come together to bring us this table. Looking deeply at the sunshine, the leaves of the tree, and the clouds, we can see the table. The one can be seen in the all, and the all can be seen in the one. One cause is never enough to bring about an effect. A cause must, at the same time, be an effect, and every effect must also be the cause of something else. Cause and effect inter-are. The idea of first and only cause, something that does not itself need a cause, cannot be applied.[6]

Thich Nhat Hanh's notion of "inter-are" speaks directly to the commandment to "love your neighbor as yourself" (Leviticus 19:18). Because all things inter-are, the notion of separate selves is one forged in ignorance. Your neighbor is your self, or, perhaps more accurately put, your neighbor and you are parts of a single "self," reality itself. This leads directly to the notion of infinite nonzero games: if there is only one "self" to which all beings belong, the only way any one being can "win" is if this "self" wins, and the only way this "self" wins is if all of its parts win as well. Right View, in other words, leads directly to the Golden Rule:

> Look where you will, there is nothing dearer to man than himself; therefore, as it is the same thing that is dear to you and to others, hurt not others with what pains yourself. (Dhammapada 5:18)[7]

> The disciple reflects: "Here I am, fond of my life, not wanting to die, fond of pleasure and averse to pain. If someone would deprive me of my life, it would not please me. If I, in turn, were to deprive another such person of his life, it would not please him. For that state unpleasing to me must be unpleasing to him; and so how could I inflict that upon him?" As a result of such reflection he abstains from taking the life of creatures and encourages others so to abstain. (Samyutta Nikaya 55:7)[8]

Perhaps intrinsic to this view is the notion of reincarnation. Given the endless nature of birth, death, and rebirth, it is only logical to imagine that any "other" in my life may have been, at one time in my past, or will be, in some time in my future, my mother, father, sister, brother, or friend and hence deserve to be treated not as an other at all but as family or, more dearly, as my self.

The Buddhist notion of self, rooted as it is in the notion of *anatman*, "no self," the denial of any permanent soul separate from the karmic process that manifests as the universe you and I experience, doesn't allow for separation between self and other. Indeed, we would be better served to speak of self-and-other or even self/other. This is why the Buddha taught that "one who loves himself should not harm another."[9]

Given the notion of "inter-are" at the heart of the Buddha's teaching, each of us intrinsically knows what it is to treat another well. In the Dhammapada, an anthology from the third century BCE of the Buddha's teachings offered on differing occasions, we find the following:

> All tremble at violence; life is dear for all. Seeing others
> as being like yourself, do not kill or cause others to kill.
> (Dhammapada 10)[10]

At the heart of Buddhist ethics are the Five Moral Precepts: abstaining from killing, theft, sexual misconduct, spreading falsehood, and fermented drinks. Regarding the first of these precepts we are taught in the Anguttara Nikaya sutra (8:39), "There is the case where a certain person, abandoning the taking of life, abstains from the taking of life. He dwells with his rod laid down, his knife laid down, scrupulous, merciful, compassionate for the welfare of all living beings."[11]

This precept seems not to matter at all in Burma, where Buddhists, even Buddhist monks, wage violent attacks on their Muslim neighbors. According to Dr. Michael Jerryson, coeditor of *Buddhist Warfare*, a 2010 exploration of Buddhist violence in Southeast Asia, "The Burmese Buddhist monks may not have initiated the violence but they rode the wave and began to incite more."[12]

Mark Juergensmeyer, coeditor of *Buddhist Warfare* and director of the Orfalea Centre for Global and International Studies at the University of Santa Barbara, California, is quoted in the same article saying, "If Islam, a religious tradition whose very name means peace, can be associated with violence [by extremists] it should be no surprise that there are angry Buddhists who become violent as well."[13]

While Dr. Juergensmeyer's logic that violent Muslims somehow explains violent Buddhists may be questionable, the fact that Buddhists will abandon their core precepts when it suits them is not.

Shaku Soen Roshi, the Zen Master who represented Buddhism as a "universal religion" at the 1897 Parliament of the World's Religions in Chicago, supported the Russo-Japanese War (1904–1905), writing:

> War is not necessarily horrible, provided that it is fought
> for a just and honorable cause, that it is fought for ... the
> upholding of humanity and civilization. Many material
> human bodies may be destroyed, many hearts broken, but
> from a broader point of view these sacrifices are so many
> phoenixes consumed in the sacred fire of spirituality.[14]

Speaking along the same lines, Zen Master Harada Daiun Sogaku (1871–1961) addressed Japanese soldiers with this advice: "[If ordered to] march: tramp, tramp, or shoot: bang, bang. This is the manifestation of the highest Wisdom [of Enlightenment]. The unity of Zen and war of which I speak extends to the farthest reaches of the holy war [now under way]."[15]

It isn't that militant Buddhists forget their precepts. Rather, it is that well-educated Buddhists use Buddhism to get around those precepts to justify the violence they want Buddhists to do. Again to cite Dr. Jerryson, "Across Buddhist tradition, intention is an exception to the rule when committing violence. If violence is seen as being a way to protect Buddhism and have pure thoughts to help or defend that, then it becomes [acceptable]."[16] As D. T. Suzuki, one of the most influential interpreters of Buddhism, especially Zen Buddhism, to the Western world wrote, "[Zen] could be wedded to anarchism or fascism, communism or democracy, atheism or idealism or any political or economic dogmatism."[17]

Nor is it the case that Buddhist violence is a uniquely modern phenomenon. In the Sinhalese Buddhist text the Mahavamsa, the Buddhist king Dutthagamani slaughters millions of people in his war against the Damil invaders. Deeply troubled by this loss of life, the king is comforted by eight *arahant*, enlightened Buddhist monks:

> From this deed arises no hindrance in thy way to heaven. Only one and a half human beings have been slain here by thee, O lord of men. The one had come unto the (three) refuges, the other had taken on himself the five precepts. Unbelievers and men of evil life were the rest, not more to be esteemed than beasts. But as for thee, thou wilt bring glory to the doctrine of the Buddha in manifold ways; therefore cast away from thy heart, O ruler of men![18]

So in Buddhism, as in Hinduism, the Golden Rule is only a rule when people want it to be.

Confucianism

As far as we know, Confucius (551–479 BCE) was the first person to have articulated the Golden Rule in writing, and it would be comforting to imagine that the philosophical system that bears his name would be a sterling example of the Rule. Sadly, this is not the case. The infinite nonzero Rule could not transform the zero-sum world of China, especially in regard to respect for women.

Living in a time of political upheaval, rampant corruption, war, and societal collapse, Confucius sought to articulate a new way of living that would set his world and his people on a path to peace and sustainability. We find his guidance in the *Analects*, a collection of the sayings of Confucius and his students compiled during the centuries following Confucius's death and coming into its current form sometime during the middle Han dynasty (206 BCE–220 CE). Regarding the Golden Rule, the *Analects* offers the following anecdote:

> Tzu-Kung asked, "In a single word, what should guide our behavior throughout our lives?" Confucius said, "*Shu* [consideration]: Do not force upon others what you would not want forced upon you." (*Analects* 2:4)

The *Analects* expands on this two chapters later. In a conversation with Tseng Tzu, a senior disciple and teacher in his own right, Confucius says, "Tseng, a single thread runs throughout my teachings, and binds them all together." Tseng Tzu agrees, and Confucius leaves the room satisfied.

The reader, of course, is left unsatisfied. What is this thread? Thankfully, Tseng Tzu's students have the same question: "What did the Master mean by this one thread? What is the thread that binds his teachings?" Tseng Tzu answered, "*Chung* [pronounced *joong*, loyalty] and *shu* [consideration]." This seems to have satisfied the students, but you and I may still wonder: what is the connection between *chung* and *shu*?

There are two notions that link *chung* and *shu*, the first etymological, the second sociological. The words *chung* and *shu*, each written with two characters, share the same lower character best translated as "heart and mind." Both *chung* and *shu*, then, are dealing with our feelings and thoughts. Where they differ is revealed in the upper character. The upper character for *chung* means "centered"; the upper character for *shu* means "compassion." The thread that runs through Confucius's teaching is the practice of centering your heart so that you have compassion for the other. This is not easily done. Indeed Confucius himself claims never to have mastered it.

> *Chung* and *shu* [loyalty and consideration] are not far from the *tao* [way]. If you do not want something inflicted upon you, then do not inflict it upon others. The morally noble adhere to four principles: what you require of your son, require of yourself in service to your father; ... what you require of your subordinate, require of yourself in service to your superior; ... what you require of your younger brother, require of yourself in service to your older brother; ... what you require of a friend, first require of yourself in relation to your friend. And I have yet to master even one of these.[19]

This is where *chung*, "loyalty," comes into play. Each person occupies a specific station in life defined by those above and those below that station. You must be true to your station by being loyal to those above and below.

The relationships between people in Confucius's philosophy are governed by sociality of place: the lower have obligations to the higher, and the higher have obligations to the lower. Over time Confucianism came to speak of the Five Relationships as essential to human flourishing:

1. Ruler and subject
2. Father and son
3. Husband and wife
4. Elder brother and younger brother
5. Friend and friend

Today we might imagine contemporary Confucians adjusting these for a more egalitarian time, but the essential message would remain the same: peace and tranquility are fostered when each person operates in accord with his or her position in the social order. This is not all that dissimilar to the Indian caste system, where what is right and just is determined not by a universal standard but by the standard applicable to one's place in the social hierarchy.

> There are four marks of the superior person, and I haven't attained even one. To honor my father, as I wish my son to honor me—I haven't achieved this. To serve my prince as I wish my minister to serve me—I haven't achieved this. To treat my elder brother as I wish my younger brother to treat me—I haven't achieved this. To respect a friend as I wish this friend would respect me—I haven't achieved this. (*Doctrine of the Mean*, chapter 13, verses 3–4)

Even if Confucius had been more successful in *chung* and *shu*, he would still not have attained harmony with the *tao*, the way of nature. *Chung* and *shu* are close to the *tao*, but not equivalent to the *tao*. There is still something missing. What is missing is *jen* (pronounced *ren*), "human kindness." While the hierarchical nature of social relationships is fixed in Confucianism, the most successful way of engaging them is not. *Jen* is not a legal system of dos and don'ts based on your place in the social hierarchy, but a spontaneous and creative engagement with another human being that seeks to uplift the relationship toward perfection. The key to this is the Golden Rule:

> A person of *jen* who cultivates moral character cultivates the moral character of others as well; a person of *jen* who seeks to be important makes others important as well; to understand others as you yourself would be understood is the cultivation of *jen*. (*Analects* 6:28)

What *jen* introduces into the practice of the Golden Rule is the capacity to put yourself in another's shoes. While *chung* and *shu* define the framework in which you operate, it is *jen* that allows you to know what to do. The Golden Rule isn't merely a matter of imposing your personal likes and dislikes on another and then acting accordingly, but rather coming to know the likes and dislikes of the other so that your actions are in accord with the other's desire rather than your own. Cultivating the imagination to see the world from the other's perspective and thus act toward the other the way the other wishes you to act is at the heart of human kindness from the Confucian perspective.

And yet it has its limits. Confucius's social hierarchy, like the Indian caste system, sets limits on the Golden Rule and the capacity of *jen* to imagine what would be literally unimaginable. An independent woman was no more welcome in Confucian society than she was in traditional Indian society governed by the Laws of Manu. And while Confucius taught us to refrain from doing unto others that which would cause suffering if done to us, Confucianism never imagined that women would want to be treated as men were treated. For example, the neo-Confucian scholar Zhu Xi (1130–1200) taught:

> To do wrong is unbecoming to a wife, and to do good is also unbecoming of a wife. A woman is merely to be obedient to what is proper. If a daughter does nothing wrong, that is enough. If she does good, then likewise, that is neither a favorable nor a desirable thing. Only spirits and food are her concern, and not to occasion sorrow to her parents is all that is called for.... And Mencius' mother said, "All a wife needs to do to fulfill her proper station in life is to prepare the five dishes, cover the wine, take care of her in-laws, and mend the clothes." Therefore a woman should bear the refinement of the inner chambers and desist from any ulterior motives.[20]

Again, the Golden Rule in and of itself is not sufficient to challenge the zero-sum nature of society, let alone transform it.

Evading the Rule in Judaism, Christianity, and Islam

In the previous chapter I looked at three Eastern religious traditions and how they articulate and then ignore the Golden Rule. I will do the same in this chapter, examining the three Abrahamic faiths. As with the last chapter, my point is not to denigrate these religions or cultures, but simply to note that the Golden Rule when articulated in a particular religion is not an independent standard of ethical behavior.

Judaism

While the command to "love your neighbor as yourself" (Leviticus 19:18) provides the basis for the Golden Rule in Judaism, a deeply rooted zero-sum tribalism makes the nonzero Golden Rule no less challenging for Judaism than it is for any other religion.

The classic expression of the Golden Rule is attributed to Rabbi Hillel (32 BCE–7 CE):

> It once happened that a certain gentile came before Shammai and said to him, "I will convert to Judaism, on condition that you teach me the whole Torah while I stand on one foot." Outraged by the request, Shammai drove the

man away with the builder's level that was in his hand. The man then went to Hillel with the same request. Hillel agreed, saying, "What is hateful to you, do not do to another. That is the entire Torah, the rest is commentary; now go and learn it." (Babylonian Talmud, *Shabbat* 31a)

While Jews often take pride in Hillel's ancient teaching, the fact that it isn't found in the Hebrew Bible should raise some questions regarding Hillel's claim that the Golden Rule is the entirety of Jewish law and teaching. You would expect, if this were so, to find some version of the Rule or some equivalent of "Love your neighbor" listed among the Ten Commandments, but you would be hard-pressed to do so; it just isn't there:

I am the Eternal your God, who brought you out of the land of Egypt, out of the house of bondage. (Exodus 20:2)

You shall have no other gods besides Me. You shall not make for yourself any graven image, nor any manner of likeness, of any thing that is in heaven above, or that is in the earth beneath, or that is in the water under the earth. You shall not bow down to them, nor serve them, for I, the Eternal your God, am a jealous God, visiting the iniquity of the parents upon the children unto the third and fourth generation of those who despise Me. (Exodus 20:3–5)

You shall not take the name of the Eternal your God in vain; for the Eternal will not hold one guiltless that takes God's name in vain. (Exodus 20:7)

Remember the Sabbath, to keep it holy. Six days you shall labor, and do all your work; but the seventh day is a Sabbath unto the Eternal your God, in it you shall not do any manner of work, you, nor your son, nor your daughter, nor your man-servant, nor your maid-servant, nor your cattle, nor the stranger that is within your gates; for in six days the Eternal made sky and earth, the sea, and all that in them is, and rested on the seventh day. Wherefore the Eternal blessed the Sabbath day, and made it holy. (Exodus 20:8–11)

Honor your father and your mother, that your days may be long upon the land that the Eternal God gives you. (Exodus 20:12)

You shall not murder. (Exodus 20:13)

You shall not commit adultery. (Exodus 20:13)

You shall not steal. (Exodus 20:13)

You shall not bear false witness against your neighbor. (Exodus 20:13)

You shall not covet your neighbor's house, nor spouse, man-servant, maid-servant, nor ox, nor ass, nor anything that is your neighbor's. (Exodus 20:14)

The Ten Commandments, of course, are not universal and are given to the Israelites alone. Perhaps that is why the Golden Rule isn't listed among them. The universal commandments according to the Rabbis of the Talmud are the Seven Laws of Noah. Yet here too the Golden Rule is absent:

Our Rabbis taught: Seven laws were given to Noah and his descendants [humanity as a whole]: establish just law courts; refrain from blasphemy, idolatry, adultery, murder, robbery, and eating flesh cut from a living animal. (Babylonian Talmud, *Sanhedrin* 56a)

If the Golden Rule were essential to Judaism, and certainly if it were the whole of Torah, as Hillel argues, you would expect it to appear in one of these lists. Yet it doesn't. It does, however, appear in extra-canonical Jewish literature that predates Hillel.

Written in the late third or early second century BCE, the book of Tobit tells the story of Tobit ("Good Guy"), an Israelite exile living in Nineveh in the eighth century BCE, who remains loyal to the God of the now sacked Temple in Jerusalem. Tobit calls his son to his side and explains what behaviors a wise and just person ought to exhibit. Among these is the Golden Rule:

> Do not withhold until tomorrow wages due today.... Stay mindful of what you do, my son, and discipline yourself in all your conduct. *What you hate, do not do to anyone.* Do not drink wine to excess or become drunk in public. Share your food with the hungry, and your clothing with the naked. Give all your surplus to charity, and do not let your desires curb your generosity. (Tobit 4:14–16)

While not everyone sees Tobit's injunctions as synonymous with the Golden Rule, there is little controversy that they are at least complementary.[1]

Having to search extra-canonical Jewish texts to find a precedent for the Rule begs the question: is Hillel's claim that the Golden Rule is the "entire Torah" a claim accepted by his peers or merely his own opinion? Searching the Talmud itself, we find another list of essentials, one in which Hillel isn't even mentioned:

> Rabbi Simlai said: Six hundred and thirteen precepts were communicated to Moses, three hundred and sixty-five negative precepts, corresponding to the number of days in the solar year, and two hundred and forty-eight positive precepts, corresponding to the number of the parts in the human body. David came and reduced these to eleven [Psalm 15].... Isaiah came and reduced them to six [Isaiah 33:25–26].... Micah came and reduced them to three [Micah 6:8], Isaiah came again and reduced them to two [Isaiah 56:1].... Amos came and reduced them to one, "For thus says the Eternal to the house of Israel: Seek Me and live" [Amos 5:4]. Rabbi Nachman ben Isaac challenged Rabbi Simlai, saying, "The meaning of 'seek Me' means to seek God through

all the commandments of Torah." Rabbi Simlai coun-
tered, saying, "Habakkuk came and also taught but one
commandment, 'The righteous shall live by faith alone'"
[Habakkuk 2:4]. (Babylonian Talmud, *Makkot* 23b–24a)

If the Golden Rule were, as the first-century Hillel taught long before
the third-century Rabbi Simlai, the "entire Torah," then why doesn't
Rabbi Simlai include it among his list of essential teachings of Judaism?
Even more interesting, why doesn't he include "Love your neighbor as
yourself"? The answer may well lie with contemporary scholar Rabbi
Jacob Neusner, who concludes that "there is no hint that the Golden
Rule is the ultimate generative rule of the Torah."[2]

Yet even if the Golden Rule were central to Jewish life, it certainly
was not definitive. To get a sense of how people work around the Golden
Rule even as they pretend to hold it sacred, let's take as a case study the
Jewish understanding of what might be called the proto–Golden Rule,
"Love your neighbor as yourself."

The full text of the biblical version of the Golden Rule reads, "Love
your neighbor as yourself; I am YHVH" (Leviticus 19:18). We will come
back to this command in a moment, but first let's juxtapose it with
another, this one from the book of Deuteronomy: "Do what is just and
good in YHVH's sight, and in this way things may go well with you, and
you will occupy the good land promised to your ancestors by YHVH
your God" (Deuteronomy 6:18).

Both texts reference YHVH, but only the second makes God the
arbiter of the good and the right. The Golden Rule in Leviticus links
the Rule to God—"I am YHVH"—but does not make God the arbiter
of what is just and good. The second text, however, implies that what
is just and good is what is "just and good in YHVH's sight." Where the
Golden Rule leaves it up to you to decide how to love your neighbor,
the commandment in Deuteronomy removes you from the equation
and demands only that you follow the guidelines set out by God or
those who legislate in the name of God.

Which is the more compelling? The answer to this question may
depend on individual taste and cannot be answered in any definitive

manner. Nevertheless, we might surmise that the author of the Leviticus passage thought the teaching to "love your neighbor" to be self-evident, since he felt no need to sweeten the pot with a promise of reward.

The reason we are to do what is just and good in YHVH's sight, on the other hand, is to earn what is right and good in our sight: things go well with us, and we come into possession of good land. The commandment in Deuteronomy applies a carrot-and-stick approach to morality: do what I say, and you will be rewarded; don't do what I say, and you will be punished.

The author of Deuteronomy points us toward God or those who legislate morality in God's name; the author of Leviticus points us toward ourselves. The way we know what is just and good in the eyes of God is to see what laws God legislates. Some of these laws are ethical, some ceremonial, and while Jewish philosophers have argued for generations whether or not the ethical and ceremonial carry equal weight (the more conservative say they do, the more liberal say they do not and hence elevate the ethical over the ceremonial), the simple fact is the Hebrew Bible itself makes no distinction between them.

All *mitzvot*—divine commandments—are equally divine and obligatory. Any distinction we may make between ethical and ceremonial commandments and any comparative weight we may assign to these categories of commandment reflect the bias of the person making the distinction and setting the weight. Thus, within the context of the Hebrew Bible, the commandment to repay the Temple priesthood 120 percent of the value of any Temple property you may have misused and to sacrifice a ram to obtain God's forgiveness (Leviticus 5:14–16) is as binding on you as the commandment to love your neighbor as yourself. Biblically speaking, the two commandments are of equal value.

But what of those cases where God commands what a normal person would consider unethical behavior? If it is God who determines what is ethical, then the point, of course, is moot. The good is what God says is good. Period. Much of Hebrew scripture follows that line of thought.

Acting as God's spokesman, Moses tells the Israelite people that when they enter the land promised to them they will obliterate the indigenous peoples—the Hittites, Girgashites, Amorites, Canaanites, Perizzites,

Hivites, and Jebusites: "You must destroy them completely; make no treaty with them, and show them no mercy" (Deuteronomy 7:1–2).

If this notion of divinely commanded genocide disturbs you—as it does me—you have to challenge the notion that God's commands are always good, right, moral, and just. You wouldn't be the first to do so.

When God reveals to Abraham his plan to wipe out all the inhabitants of Sodom, Abraham confronts God over the immorality of such an act:

> "You plan to obliterate the just along with the unjust?...
> You can't do such a thing, slaughtering the righteous
> along with the wicked, treating the good and the bad as
> if they were the same. You can't do this! Shouldn't the
> Judge of all the earth do justly?" (Genesis 18:23–25)

In this story Abraham explicitly denies the notion that God's commands are intrinsically moral and just. On the contrary, justice trumps God. Saying that God, as Judge, must do justly elevates justice above God. According to Abraham, justice must bind God, and justice, not God, determines what is right and good. And who determines what is just? Abraham! This is the meaning of Abraham's debate with God over how many righteous people must reside in Sodom for God to spare the city. Abraham begins with fifty and bargains with God until they settle on ten. Justice is now defined—by Abraham—as sparing the city if ten good people reside there (Genesis 18:24–32).

What Abraham does in this story—elevating human justice over God's might—is central to our understanding of the Golden Rule. While the command to "love your neighbor as yourself" is linked to God by the phrase that follows it—"I am YHVH"—the phrase itself tells us nothing about how we are to love. The standard is not set by God and is hence left up to human interpretation.

Years after Abraham's defeat of God and God's notion of justice (killing the innocent along with the guilty), God speaks to Abraham again, this time commanding him to sacrifice his son Isaac on Mount Moriah (Genesis 22:2). Given Abraham's concern for the people of Sodom, we would expect him to protest. On the contrary, without saying a word, Abraham rushes off the next morning to fulfill God's command.

In the earlier tale, Abraham questions divine authority and sets a human standard for justice. In the latter tale, Abraham never questions the ethics of God and seems to have no moral standard of his own against which to measure it.

The nineteenth-century philosopher Søren Kierkegaard (1813–1855) writes passionately about the near sacrifice of Isaac in his book *Fear and Trembling*. His argument is that Abraham trusted in God to do what was right even though it appears that God is asking him to do what is wrong. Kierkegaard speaks of what he calls the "teleological suspension of the ethical."[3]

Teleology is the notion that there exists a *telos*, or final cause, that justifies actions taken in fulfillment of that cause. Abraham was acting faithfully, trusting that God is driven by final causes that must be just. In other words, Abraham will do what he is commanded to do, always trusting that in the end God will not act in an unjust manner. Given his encounter with God at Sodom, Abraham has no basis on which to base this hope. Nevertheless, he seems to act on it.

The Golden Rule and the command to "love your neighbor as yourself" take God out of the equation. God has nothing to do with this. Even though the teaching to love your neighbor is followed by the phrase "I am YHVH," this phrase adds nothing to our understanding of the command to love our neighbor.

Rabbi Moses ben Nahman (1194–1270), the thirteenth-century Spanish rabbi known as Ramban, claimed in his commentary on Leviticus 19:18 that the phrase "as yourself" is an exaggeration. The human heart, he explains, is "incapable of loving another to the same degree" as oneself. This is why, Ramban explains, the commandment isn't about the heart at all, but the head. You cannot feel equally for all, but you can use your intellect and reason to shape your behavior in a way that it serves the welfare of all as you understand it. In other words, you shall seek the welfare of others in every aspect of their lives, just as you seek your own welfare in every aspect of your life.

Given this understanding of the text, the idea of love is not emotional but rational. What you love, according to the Ramban, isn't your neighbor per se but those things that contribute to your neighbor's welfare.

The Hebrew text itself makes this clear. If the Hebrew Bible meant to say "Love your neighbor as yourself," then the Hebrew would read *V'ahavta et rei'acha kamocha*, with the word *et* linking "you shall love" (*ahavta*) to "your neighbor" (*rei'acha*). The text actually says something different: *V'ahavta l'rei'acha kamocha*, which is more accurately translated as "You shall love [*ahavta*] for [*l'*] your neighbor [*rei'acha*) what you love for yourself [*kamocha*]."[4] The command is not "Love your neighbor," but "Assist your neighbor to succeed in all the ways that you wish to succeed."

Commandments are behavioral. The Hebrew Bible is commanding not a feeling but an action. Thus with regard to wealth, you must support those things that will allow your neighbor to become wealthy and resist those things that would limit his ability to do so, just as you would support those things that allow you to pursue wealth and resist those things that inhibit you from doing so.

Here is how the nineteenth-century rabbi Samson Raphael Hirsch puts it:

> The term [*l'rei'acha*] (lit., "to your neighbor") refers not to the personality of the other, but to everything that pertains to his personality: all the circumstances that determine his position in life, for better or for worse. To these we are to direct our love. We are to seek his welfare, just as we seek our own welfare. We are to rejoice in his happiness as though it were our own, grieve over his sorrow as though it were our own, assist eagerly in advancing his welfare as though it were our own, and keep trouble away from him as though we ourselves were threatened by it. This is a requirement that we can fulfill even in connection with a person with whom we have no affinity.[5]

Given these readings of Leviticus 19:18, we would expect religious people to be more just, kind, and loving than secular people. Yet this is hardly the case.

> To be sure, religious folks have sat through hundreds of sermons admonishing them to "love thy neighbor as

thyself" and to "do unto others as you would have them do unto you." On the other hand, in many parts of the world religion is linked to intolerance, violence, and mayhem—not to civic good manners. As the seventeenth-century French philosopher Blaise Pascal said, reflecting on the religious wars in his era, "Men never do evil so completely and cheerfully as when they do it from religious conviction."[6]

Why is this so? Again look to our model of finite and infinite games.

When it comes to the finite zero-sum game of religious correctness—whose God is the real God, whose faith is the truth faith—the goal is to win at the expense of the other. As political scientist Robert Putnam's research shows, "theology and piety have very little to do with ... neighborliness," and yet everything to do with intolerance and lack of support for the civil rights of those who believe differently than you do.[7]

Christianity

It is commonplace to link Jesus with the Golden Rule, yet the Rule is found in only two lines in the Gospels: "In everything do to others as you would have them do to you; for this is the law and the prophets" (Matthew 7:12, NRSV); and "Do to others as you would have others do to you" (Luke 6:31). Neither Mark, chronologically the first Gospel, nor John, the last Gospel, have Jesus teaching the Golden Rule.

Just as we noticed that the Golden Rule as such is absent from both the Ten Commandments and the Seven Laws of Noah, so it is absent from Jesus's Beatitudes, what some take to be the central articulation of what it is to be a Christian:

> Blessed are the poor in spirit, for theirs is the kingdom of
>   heaven.
> Blessed are those who mourn, for they shall be comforted.
> Blessed are the meek, for they shall inherit the earth.
> Blessed are those who hunger and thirst for righteousness,
>   for they shall be filled.

> Blessed are the merciful, for they shall be shown mercy.
>
> Blessed are the pure in heart, for they shall see God.
>
> Blessed are the peacemakers, for they shall be called children of God.
>
> Blessed are those who are persecuted because of righteousness, for theirs is the kingdom of heaven.
>
> Blessed are you when people insult you, persecute you and falsely say all kinds of evil against you because of me.
>
> Rejoice and be glad, because great is your reward in heaven, for in the same way they persecuted the prophets who were before you. (Matthew 5:2–12, NIV)

When Jesus does present the Golden Rule two chapters later in Matthew, he adds an element lacking from that of his elder Hillel. To understand what this is, you have to read the passage in context:

> Do not judge, or you too will be judged. And in the same way you judge others, you will be judged, and with the measure you use, it will be measured to you.... Which of you, if your child asks for bread, will provide a stone? Or if your child asks for a fish, will offer a snake? If you, then, though you are evil, know how to provide well for your children, how much more will your Father in heaven provide well for those who ask him! Therefore in everything, do to others what you would have them do to you, for this sums up the Law and the Prophets. (Matthew 7:1–12)

At first Jesus sounds as if he is echoing Hillel: "What is hateful to you do not do to another. That is the entire Torah." He may be. But the Gospels place the teaching in a context far different from that of Hillel.

As the Gospel of Matthew makes clear, Jesus is offering the Golden Rule not as a way to treat others for righteousness sake alone, but as a way of avoiding negative judgment by God.

So in the afterlife we'll receive the same treatment that we've given others. When Mt 7:12 says, "Therefore, treat others as you want to be treated," the "therefore" hints at an ends-means argument: if you want a certain treatment yourself, then, to get this, you must treat others that way too. It may disappoint that Jesus appeals to self-interest (reward and punishment) instead of something higher (like unselfish love for God and neighbor). But the gospels have to appeal to a wide range of people and thus provide lower motives as well as higher ones.[8]

What philosophy professor Harry Gensler calls "lower" and "higher" we are calling zero-sum and nonzero. In a zero-sum game of winners and losers, it is better to be a winner, and if the Golden Rule is how you win this game, then the Golden Rule is how you will play it. As we have seen, however, the Golden Rule doesn't operate well in finite zero-sum games, a fact that may explain why, when religions appeal to the "lower motives" of people, they often do so in violation of the Golden Rule.

Just then a rabbi rose to question Jesus. "Rabbi," he said, "what must I do to inherit eternal life?" Jesus replied, "Consult Torah; what do you read there?" The man answered, "You shall love the Eternal your God with all your heart, and with every breath, and with all your strength, and with all your mind; and your neighbor as yourself." And he said to him, "You are correct! Do as instructed, and you will live." (Luke 10:25–28)

The reason we are to follow the Hebrew Bible's dictates to love God and love our neighbor is to earn eternal life in heaven and, by extension, avoid eternal torment in hell. Jesus is on firm Jewish ground here. Just prior to the admonition to love God in Deuteronomy 6:4, we are told why we are to love God: "Pay attention, Israel, and observe these commandments carefully in order that life goes well for you, and your numbers grow in a land of milk and honey, as the Eternal God of your ancestors has promised you" (Deuteronomy 6:3).

While it is true that Leviticus 19:18, "Love your neighbor as yourself," does not place this commandment in an *if-then* context (if you love your neighbor, then you will reap a reward), it isn't too hard to imagine most people hearing the commandment in that context. Finite zero-sum games are the norm for most of us, which is why the Golden Rule, though ubiquitous, is so little followed.

Among the clearest articulations of a finite zero-sum game, and yet one that actually contains its own transformation to an infinite nonzero game, is presented to the apostles by Jesus later in Matthew 25. After revealing privately to the apostles the trials that await them, Jesus, perhaps in an attempt to comfort them, reveals the end-times as well:

> The Son of Man, surrounded by angels, will arrive in glory and take his place on his glorious throne. Before will gather all the nations, and he will separate the people one from another as a shepherd separates sheep from goats. He will put the sheep on his right and the goats on his left.
>
> To those on his right he will say, "You who are blessed by my Father; come and take your inheritance: the kingdom prepared for you from the moment of creation. For you fed me when I was hungry, and slaked my thirst when I was thirsty, and offered me hospitality when I was a stranger, and clothed me when I was naked, and nursed me when I was ill, and visited me when I was imprisoned."
>
> Confused, the righteous will ask, "When did we feed you, or offer you drink, or welcome you into our homes, or clothe you, or nurse you to health, or comfort you in prison?"
>
> The King will reply to them, "Here is the truth: whatever you do for the least among you, you do for me."
>
> Turning to those on his left he will say, "Get away from me cursed ones, into the eternal fire prepared for the devil and his angels. For you ignored me when I was hungry, and when I was thirsty you gave me nothing to drink. You denied me hospitality when I was a stranger.

When I was naked you didn't clothe me. When I was sick and in prison you did nothing to care for me."

No less confused than the righteous, the accursed will ask, "Lord, when did we see you hungry or thirsty or a stranger or in need of clothes or sick or in prison, and did not help you?"

And as before he will reply, "Here is the truth: whatever you did not do for the least among you, you did not do for me."

Then the accursed will go to eternal punishment, and the righteous to eternal life. (Matthew 25:31–46)

The notion of sheep and goats, eternal winners and losers, is a stark articulation of a finite zero-sum game. But Jesus plays with the format so dramatically that "those with ears to hear" might be led to living an infinite nonzero game instead.

The key is how you win the game. Winning is achieved not by adhering to some set of commandments, but by seeing all people, from the highest to the lowest, as the Son of Man. This undermines all notions of caste, class, gender, and the like. Everyone is the Son of Man and deserves to be treated as such. If dividing people into sheep and goats is pure finite zero-sum thinking, then seeing both sheep and goats as Christ is pure infinite nonzero thinking. The latter erases the former, which, I suggest, was the plan of the teaching all along: lure the people in with the game they know, and then turn things upside down with the game they don't know but that is key to the vision of Jesus.

Jesus does something similar in the parable of the Good Samaritan (Luke 10:25–28). The Jews in Jesus's time despised the Samaritans as their chief rivals. Samaritans claim to be descendants of the tribes of Ephraim and Manasseh, as well as the tribe of Levi, from which the Temple priests are chosen. Samaritanism claims, contra Judaism, to be the authentic religion of Abraham, has its own version of Torah, and insists that it rather than Judaism is the true religion of the pre-exilic Israelites. As we know from Jesus's conversation with the Samaritan woman at the well, the Samaritans worship on their own mountain, while Jews worship on the Temple Mount (John 4:20). Although Jesus insists that Judaism is superior to Samaritanism ("Salvation is from the Jews"; John 4:22, NRSV), he foretells a time soon coming when all such zero-sum religions will give way to something new: "Yet a time is coming and has now come when the true worshipers will worship the Father in the Spirit and in truth, for they are the kind of worshipers the Father seeks" (John 4:23, NIV).

By making the Samaritan the hero of the Good Samaritan parable— by making him the neighbor we are to love—Jesus is challenging his people to expand their minds, to move beyond a zero-sum us/them worldview to something more inclusive and nonzero. It will take the apostle Paul to make this explicit: "There is neither Jew nor gentile, neither slave nor free, nor is there male and female, for you are all one and the same in Christ Jesus" (Galatians 3:28).

Jesus does something similar when he expands not the definition of neighbor but the definition of love in Matthew 5:

> You have been taught, "Love your neighbor and hate your enemy." But I teach differently: love your enemies and pray for those who persecute you, for in this way you will become children of your heavenly Father. God causes the sun to rise on both the evil and on the good, and sends rain to fall on both the just and on the unjust. There is nothing special about loving those who love you; even the tax collectors do that. There is nothing special in greeting only your brothers and sisters; even the gentiles do that. Rather, be perfect as your heavenly Father is perfect. (Matthew 5:43–48)

The Gospel writer is mistaken that the Hebrew Bible teaches you to "hate your enemy," but this doesn't diminish the message Jesus offers in this text. The teaching asks an unasked question: How do we become perfect as God is perfect?

The question is new because Judaism doesn't ask for perfection, only holiness: "Be holy, as I the Eternal God am holy" (Leviticus 19:2). Holiness is defined in the Hebrew Bible by the many commandments set by God. Jesus's notion of perfection is new and begs for a definition. Jesus provides it: loving your neighbor and praying for you neighbor is what it takes to be perfect.

Fair enough, but why does Jesus bother with the notion that the sun rises and the rain falls on everyone regardless of their morality? While any answer to this is speculative, it is worth our effort to speculate, because it gives us further insight into Jesus's use of the Golden Rule.

> If you follow God's every commandment that I [Moses] am commanding you today—to love and serve the Eternal God with all your heart, with every breath—then God will water your land with the seasonal rains, early and late, and you will harvest in your grain, wine, and oil. Your fields will yield grasses for your cattle, and you will eat and be satisfied. But if you are seduced by other gods, and turn away to worship them, the Eternal's anger will flare up against you. The skies will close up, no rain will fall, your fields will be barren, and you will quickly die even here in this good land the Eternal is giving you. (Deuteronomy 11:13–17)

The Hebrew Bible is setting forth its own zero-sum game: do as God says and win; refuse to do as God says and lose. Jesus isn't abandoning the zero-sum paradigm entirely, but he is moving the goalposts. While the Hebrew Bible places winning and losing in this world, Jesus says the rains prove nothing. Dawn comes for everyone. The rains, when they fall, have nothing to do with morality—the wicked as well as the just benefit. So where is the game won and lost? In the next life. Loving your neighbor—the Samaritan as well as the Jew, and by extension the Roman as well—will not determine the weather, but it will determine whether or not you get into heaven.

Where the Hebrew Bible is concerned with this life, Jesus is concerned with the next. And yet in these cases both support the finite zero-sum game model. When we look away from the afterlife and toward the kingdom of heaven on earth, however, we find something quite different.

In the Lord's Prayer Jesus teaches us to pray for the day when God's kingdom will arrive and the will of God be done "on earth as it is in heaven" (Matthew 6:10, NRSV). But just what is the will of God?

Let me suggest just one parable that speaks to this profoundly and that makes the shift from finite zero-sum thinking to infinite nonzero thinking: the parable of the landowner and the vineyard:

> The kingdom of heaven is like a landowner who went out at dawn to hire day workers to harvest his grapes. He settled on a price for their labor and set them to work. He hired more workers mid-morning, again at noon, and again in mid- and late afternoon. At the end of the day the land-lord called the workers together and paid each of them the amount agreed to by the workers hired at dawn, a decision that upset the longer-working laborers. "We worked longer," they argued, "and hence deserve more by way of compensation." The landlord replied, "You are getting what you agreed to; there is nothing unfair here at all. If I choose to pay the last workers the same as the first, that is my affair, not yours." Jesus then caps the parable with this: "Thus the last will be first and the first will be last." (Matthew 20:1–16)

This is a wonderful nonzero parable and deserves careful unpacking. First, it is important to note that it is the landowner who is like the kingdom of heaven. Often people imagine the kingdom of heaven is the vineyard in which all are paid equally for the same work, no matter how long they work. But Jesus explicitly states that it is the landlord that is like the kingdom and not the vineyard. This means that the kingdom of heaven isn't a state of being, but a way of acting. And the action it requires reflects the Golden Rule.

What does the worker hired at dusk desire? That he or she was hired at dawn and could reap the benefits of a full day's work. What does the landowner do? He does unto them just what they desire: he pays them for a full day's work even though they worked only part of the day.

But what about the desires of the all-day laborers? They were not cheated, but when they saw the generosity extended to the others by the landowner, they wanted it extended to themselves as well. In other words, they interpreted the entire exchange from the zero-sum perspective of a finite game. Viewed this way, it doesn't seem all that fair.

The landowner, however, is acting on a different premise, a nonzero premise, what Jesus called the kingdom of heaven. The kingdom of heaven, which Jesus prays will be the norm on earth as it is in heaven— "Your kingdom come, Your will be done, on earth as it is heaven" (Matthew 6:10, NRSV)—is an infinite nonzero game. This is why everyone receives the same wage. Fairness has nothing to do with it; this is all about infinite abundance.

Imagine you and a friend go swimming in the Atlantic Ocean. Your friend jumps in as soon as you arrive, but taking advantage of the sun and finding the water a bit too chilly, you opt not to go swimming until later in the day. When you do jump in, do you receive less of the ocean than does your friend? True, you get to enjoy swimming in the ocean for a shorter period of time, but the ocean is yours to enjoy no less that it is for your friend. This is infinite abundance. Because it is infinite, everyone gets it all.

Such a game ends all finite zero-sum play. Hence Jesus's capping phrase: "Thus the first will be last and the last will be first" (Matthew 20:16). The goal of a finite game is to be first, and being first necessitates that others are last. In the kingdom of heaven, however, things are different. Do not read Jesus as saying that in the kingdom of heaven the winners now will be losers then, and the losers now will be winners then. This is still finite zero-sum thinking. In the kingdom of heaven on earth there will be no losers, and hence no winners either.

In the kingdom of heaven, the first will be last, but being last they will become first. Of course being first only makes them last once again, and that only makes them first, and on and on until at last the listener with "ears to hear" (Matthew 11:15) will realize that all such talk of winners and losers has no place in the infinite nonzero world of God's kingdom. Jesus imagines a time when the entire zero-sum worldview of first and last is over—not reversed but ended.

In other words, the kingdom of God is like a person who acts in such a way as to shatter zero-sum thinking and the finite games that arise from it. And that is precisely what the Golden Rule does.

Of course focusing on the teachings of Jesus alone might give the impression that Christianity, unlike the other religions we have so far examined, is free of ignoring the Golden Rule when it suits its purposes. This is far from the case; take the Inquisition for example.

Pope Innocent IV authorized the use of torture to get heretics to confess their false beliefs, and by the middle of the thirteenth century inquisitors were absolved of any sin they might accrue when torturing their victims. Two hundred years later, all pretense of using torture to elicit confessions was dropped, and the *Directorium Inquisitorum*, a handbook for church inquisitors produced in 1578, states that the purpose of torture is not "for the correction and good of the person punished, but for the public good in order that others may become terrified and weaned away from the evils they would commit."[9]

And then there is the explicit Jew-hatred that marks the history of Christianity. Just take Martin Luther as our example of a man steeped in the nonzero ideals of Jesus and yet incapable of seeing how these might be in conflict with his zero-sum attitude toward Jews:

> What then shall we Christians do with this damned, rejected race of Jews?... First set fire to their synagogues and schools.... This is to be done in honor of our Lord and of Christendom, so that God might see that we are Christians.... Second, I advise that their houses also be razed and destroyed.... Third, I advise that all their prayer books and Talmudic writings, in which such idolatry, lies, cursing and blasphemy are taught, be taken from them.... Fourth, I advise that their rabbis be forbidden to teach.... Fifth, I advise that safe-conduct on the highways be abolished completely for the Jews.[10]

Islam

Islam, like every other religion, articulates a version of the Golden Rule and then proceeds to ignore it when doing so suits the situation at hand. The evils of Islamic tribalism and its zero-sum worldview is so ubiquitous today that even mentioning it is considered by some to be an act of political incorrectness at best and hate speech at worst. But the whole point of this book is to point out that the Golden Rule and the nonzero worldview it promotes is in fact antithetical to the zero-sum worldview that continues to shape humanity and influence religion.

Islam begins with the revelation of the Qur'an (literally "Reading" or "Recitation") to Muhammad via the angel Gabriel in the year 610 CE. The term *Islam* is derived from the root *s-l-m*, often associated with *salaam* (peace), but better understood as voluntary submission to the will of Allah.[11] While the Qur'an is the essential text of Islam, and the final revelation of God to humanity, Muslims also esteem the Hadith (tradition), the sayings and acts of the Prophet Muhammad (PBUH) compiled long after the death of the Prophet himself.

The Golden Rule as such doesn't appear in the Qur'an, but the Qur'an does come close: "Be good to your parents, to relatives, to orphans, to the needy, to neighbors near and far, to travelers in need, and to your slaves" (Qur'an 4:36);[12] "Woe to those who give short measure, who demand of other people full measure for themselves, but give less than they should when it is they who weigh or measure for others" (Qur'an 83:1–3).[13]

It is in the Hadith, the sayings and acts of the Prophet Muhammad, that we find the Islamic Golden Rule. In the *Sahih Muslim*, a compilation of sayings of the Prophet published by the ninth-century Muslim Abdul Husain Muslim bin al-Hajjaj, we find the following:

> We have it on the authority of the Prophet's companion Anas ibn Malik that the Prophet (PBUH) taught: By Him who holds my life in His hands, not one of you is truly faithful unless he desires for his neighbor or his brother what he desires for himself. (*Sahih Muslim*, book 1, number 72)

Given the language of the Hadith, we might wonder how expansively we are to take the notion of "brother" and "neighbor." The thirteenth-century Muslim scholar an-Nawawi explains this as follows:

> It is better to interpret this as brotherhood in general, such that it includes the disbeliever and the Muslim. So

he should love for his brother, the disbeliever, what he loves for himself which is his entering Islam, just as he should love for his brother Muslim that he remains in Islam. For this reason, it is recommended to supplicate for the disbeliever to be guided. The meaning of love here is an intention for good and benefit, and this meaning is religious love, not human love. (*Sharh Arba'een An-Nawawi*, Hadith number 13)[14]

I cite this passage for two reasons. First, it allows us to read "brother" and "neighbor" more expansively. Second, it shows us yet again the limits of the Golden Rule. When what I desire becomes the criteria for what you *ought* to desire, the Golden Rule is no longer operating in an infinite nonzero way. On the contrary, as an-Nawawi makes clear, since I cannot imagine anything better for myself than to be and remain a Muslim, I cannot imagine anything better for you than this as well. Hence it only makes sense that my loving you as I want you to love me must result in my efforts to make and keep you a Muslim.

As we have seen, the ability to use the Golden Rule to sanction what I as a non-Muslim would categorize as an intrusion into my private life and to engage in behavior toward me that I clearly do not desire is not unique to Islam. The Rule is only valid as an ethical guide in the context of infinite nonzero exchanges, something religions are not all that keen on promoting.

This becomes all the more clear in the following Hadith, where true belief is tied not to Islam per se but to universal love and peace:

> Paradise is closed to you unless you believe, and you do not believe until you love one another. What does it mean to love one another? Spread peace among yourselves. (*Sahih Muslim*, book 1, number 96)

And yet for every universal statement we can find one more parochial:

> Love for the Muslims, the believers, and the people of your house what you love for yourself; and hate for them and the people of your house what you hate for yourself,

and then you will be a believer; be a good neighbor to whomever will be your neighbor among the people and you will be a Muslim. (*Al-Bayhaqi*, Shu'b Al-Iman, number 10369, Sahih)[15]

My point isn't to single out Islam for criticism; indeed the same criticisms have been made regarding all religions. My point is that the Golden Rule, like every rule, is open to interpretation, and the quality of that interpretation will depend on one's worldview and the type of game that worldview promotes. If your worldview is finite and zero-sum, a game of us *versus* them is inevitable, and the Golden Rule will extend only to us and not to them. If your worldview is infinite and nonzero, a game of us *and* them, then the Golden Rule is the finest guide to successful play.

In his essay "The Golden Rule in Islam,"[16] Thomas Emil Homerin of the University of Rochester offers two very different understandings of the Golden Rule that speak to the worlds of finite and infinite games. He begins with a quote from Osama Bin Laden's apologetic titled *Messages to the World*:

> There is a lesson in what is happening in occupied Palestine, and what happened on September 11, [2001] and [in Spain] on March 11, [2004] [namely that] your goods are returned to you.... In what creed are your dead considered innocent but ours worthless? By what logic does your blood count as real and ours no more than water? Reciprocal treatment is part of justice ... therefore stop spilling our blood to save your own.... For we only killed Russians after they invaded Afghanistan and Chechnya, we only killed Europeans after they invaded Afghanistan and Iraq, and we only killed Americans in New York after they supported the Jews in Palestine and invaded the Arabian peninsula.[17]

Bin Laden's ethic is "do unto others as they have done unto you." This is an ethic of reciprocity much closer to the biblical "an eye for an eye" (Exodus 21:24) and very different from the Golden Rule or "love your neighbor as yourself" (Leviticus 19:18). For Bin Laden, morality is reactive rather than proactive, whereas the Golden Rule is proactive: regardless of what the other does to you, do to the other only that which you would want done to you.

Fearing that Islam is being painted with the violent reactive morality of Bin Laden, Professor Homerin draws our attention to "A Common Word between Us," a letter sent to Pope Benedict XVI and other Christian leaders, and signed by "over 125 Muslim clerics and scholars from around the world [affirming] that the common beliefs held by Jews, Christians, and Muslims in 'the love of one God, and love of the neighbor' should serve as 'a basis for peace and understanding.'"[18] The idea is that Muslims, along with Jews and Christians, place the Golden Rule at the heart of their respective faiths and thus should be able to find common ground and establish peace among them based on it.

As we have seen, however, the fact that the Golden Rule can be found in each of these faiths—as well as others—in no way proves that it is central to any of them. Nevertheless, as a means of shifting us from finite zero-sum thinking to infinite nonzero thinking, the Golden Rule has no rival, and if these Muslim leaders can use the Golden Rule to make this shift among Jews, Christians, and Muslims—more power to them.

However, I read "A Common Word between Us" closely and found that despite Professor Homerin's claim to the contrary, the "us" in this letter does not include the Jews at all, let alone any other religion. While mention is made of the "Old Testament" and "Jewish liturgy" and numerous citations from the Hebrew Bible are referenced, these are all done in the context of Christianity and Jesus, with almost no mention of Jews and Judaism.

One might note that because this letter was addressed to Christian and not Jewish leaders the fact that its scope is limited should not surprise us, but even within the frame of Muslim-Christian dialogue, "A Common Word between Us" is far from an infinite nonzero game. The letter says:

> As Muslims, and in obedience to the Holy Qur'an, we
> ask Christians to come together with us on the common

essentials of our two religions ... that we shall worship none but God, and that we shall ascribe no partner unto Him, and that none of us shall take others for lords beside God.... Let this common ground be the basis of all future interfaith dialogue between us.[19]

This "common ground" is in fact a rejection of Christianity. When the letter urges us to worship "none but God," it denies the Trinity. When it asks that we "ascribe no partner" to God, it denies the Second Person of that Trinity, as it does with its injunction of taking "others for lords." Yet again the game religion plays is finite and zero-sum.

It Comes Down to Interpretation

This brief look at the Golden Rule tells us only one thing: the Golden Rule is ubiquitous. But does this matter? Many people think it does, and they celebrate the ubiquity of the Golden Rule as proof that it is *the* universal guiding principle that can unite all humanity in a single ethical family.[20] My understanding is different.

For me, the importance of the Golden Rule depends on the type of game you are playing. A finite zero-sum game interprets the Golden Rule in a way that furthers injustice and violence; an infinite nonzero game interprets the Rule in a way that holds out the promise of universal justice, compassion, and peace.

5

What Have We Learned?

Is God Necessary for Morality?

God is no hedge against evil. On the contrary, the God of a finite zero-sum game is often the catalyst for evil. So why is it that religions root their morality in a God or some other transcendent principle to which people are to subsume themselves?

There are, I think, two reasons for this. First, religion is a cultural artifact, a narrative created by humans for the benefit of believers. By in large religion is rooted in zero-sum thinking and the world of finite games. The religious see their religion as superior to and often in competition with others. This is true of most religions, and not only those arising from the monotheism of the Middle East. While Judaism, Christianity, and Islam may be the bloodiest religions we humans have created, the morality of Hinduism and Buddhism, especially with regard to caste and women, is not unblemished. And wherever religion becomes entangled with the state, it is rarely reticent to fan the flames of war.

The second reason religions root their moral systems in God or the transcendent is that they often demand actions of people who, if not for the command of a superior power, would almost never agree to do them.

Most people today are spontaneously moral: the idea of torturing or killing another human being is deeply traumatic for them. So, in order to make them do it, a larger "sacred" Cause is needed, something that makes petty individual concerns about killing seem trivial. Religion or ethnic belonging fit this role perfectly. There are, of course, cases of pathological atheists who are able to commit mass murder just for pleasure, just for the sake of it, but they are rare exceptions. The majority needs to be anaesthetized against their elementary sensitivity to another's suffering. For this, a sacred Cause is needed: without this Cause, we would have to feel all the burden of what we did, with no Absolute on whom to put the ultimate responsibility.

Religious ideologists usually claim that, true or not, religion makes some otherwise bad people do some good things. From today's experience, however, one should rather stick to Steven Weinberg's claim: while, without religion, good people would have been doing good things and bad people bad things, only religion can make good people do bad things.[1]

My aim here is not to say that religions are intrinsically violent, but simply to provide examples in support of the idea that God or some other transcendent ideal is not necessarily the source of moral good, nor a bulwark against evil. On the contrary, great evil—evil that you and I would shun if we thought about it rationally for even a moment—is done in the name of God.

This argument isn't new, of course, and those who seek to defend religion often cite the evils of Hitler. The problem with this ploy is that Adolf Hitler saw himself as a prophet of God and saw Nazism as the work of God.

> In *Mein Kampf* Hitler wrote that "faith is often the sole foundation of a moral attitude" and that "various substitutes have not proved so successful from the standpoint of results that they could be regarded as useful replacement

for previous religious creeds." ... Hitler's most famous statement on the subject was made in his Reischstag speech of 1938, when he proclaimed: "I believe today that I am acting in the sense of the Almighty/creator. By warding off the Jews I am fighting for the Lord's work."[2]

Four years prior to Hitler's 1938 speech, Professor Ernst Bergmann wrote a catechism for the new Positive Christianity of Nazism that included a direct rejection of atheism: "The German religion is a religion of the people. It has nothing in common with free thought, atheist propaganda, and the breakdown of current religions."[3]

Of course normative Christians of any denomination will no doubt condemn Hitler's Positive Christianity, but that's beside the point. This makes clear that evil done in the name of God is at least as horrible as evil done in the name of systems of thought that had no use for God whatsoever.

Turning one's moral judgments over to God is no guarantee of doing what is right. Although it is commonplace for people of faith to insist that they are avoiding doing what they want, and only doing what God wants—"not my will but Your will be done" (Luke 22:42)—there is no way to avoid the human element even in matters of faith. Simply put, God is no hedge against evil:

> The fact that the twentieth century was the bloodiest century in human history (by raw numbers only, not by percentage of population casualties) has nothing whatsoever to do with a lack of religious or moral values (which, clearly, were not lacking). Given the killing technologies of modern states (and their correspondingly larger populations) there is little doubt that the crusades, inquisitions, and religious wars of the medieval and early modern periods would have easily produced the vast killing fields of our time. The problem is not a lack of God, religion, or morals.[4]

The problem is the nature of intrinsically violent finite zero-sum games. What matters isn't the cause—religious or secular—that sanctions evil, but the worldview that cause reflects. When Shia Muslims and Sunni Muslims murder each other, they do so in the name of the same God. But what allows them to believe in a murderous God is not Allah himself, who in other settings is All-Merciful and All-Compassionate, but the finite zero-sum game that Shia and Sunni Muslims play. Only one of them can be right; only one can be the true Islam, and the only way to prove that you are that one is to defeat if not exterminate the competition.

It is the game and not the God or cause that determines what is good and just. When the game is finite and zero-sum, what is good and just is what obliterates your enemy.

If your game is finite and your worldview zero-sum, then your God or cause will sanction violence and perhaps even genocide. What Hitler sought do to the Jews was nothing other than what the Israelites did to the indigenous peoples of Canaan. Hitler convinced people to cleanse the world of Jews in the name of his God; Moses convinced people to cleanse the Promised Land of its natives in the name of his God. The name doesn't matter. What matters is the capacity to motivate people to do unspeakable evil by invoking a power greater than themselves, be it God, the state, or some other cause.

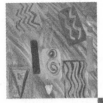

6

What's Love Got to Do with It?

The Golden Rule and Reciprocity

Earlier we cited the spiritual teacher Florence Scovel Shinn's notion that life is a "great game of giving and receiving." Many students of the Golden Rule see it in just this way: as an affirmation of ethical reciprocity. In this chapter we will explore the validity of this notion and hopefully convince you that the Golden Rule is something else entirely: not a rule of reciprocity but a rule that shatters reciprocity in favor of a greater sense of nonduality and nonzero play. But let us begin with the idea of reciprocity and see where it takes us.

> The Golden Rule is an abstract mandate to use an ethic of reciprocity as the fundamental guide to the way we consider, conceive, carry out, and assess our actions toward other people. The Golden Rule does not discuss particular actions, nor does it guarantee rewards for following it. Rather, it prescribes reciprocity as the foundational conceptual framework and context of consistency for shaping and evaluating our actions toward others.[1]

One reason why the Golden Rule doesn't prescribe specific actions is because it is a principle rather than a law. That is to say, it is a means by which you evaluate and choose among various actions open to you. The Golden Rule doesn't tell you what to do but how to decide what to do. But does it place this decision in the realm of reciprocity?

Reciprocity is a quality of exchange between parties. Put bluntly, it is a matter of tit for tat, or doing to others as others are doing to you. Certainly you may negotiate with the other so that what is done to you is something you value being done to you, and what you do to the other is something the other values as well, but as we shall see, reciprocity is not limited to positive exchange. But is reciprocity at the heart of the Golden Rule?

Placing reciprocity at the heart of the Golden Rule actually shifts the focus of the Rule from you to the other. Neither "Do to others as you would have them do to you " nor "Do not do to others as you would have them not do to you" requires you to determine what the other values. The standard for setting value is what you want or do not want, and not what the other wants or does not want. There is no reciprocity here. If anything, there is a profound selfishness: your likes and dislikes are the arbiters of what is right and just.

The fact that the Golden Rule doesn't promote specific actions and that it makes your preferences the determining factor in deciding what actions to follow and what actions to avoid leads some interpreters of the Rule to see it as anything but a viable or valuable principle.

> The Golden Rule is not really a very good guide to con-
> duct.... If followed literally, and how else are we to under-
> stand it, it requires all normal policemen not to arrest
> criminals, and all normal judges not to sentence them.
> Assuming that normal judges and policemen want neither
> to be caught nor sentenced, according to the Golden Rule,
> it follows that they ought not to arrest or sentence oth-
> ers.... So it now seems that the Golden Rule is really pretty
> useless if you are trying to find out what you ought to do.[2]

One might, of course, counter this argument by suggesting that the Rule is not to be taken literally, but then how should it be taken? If the Golden Rule doesn't mean what it says, then what does it mean?

The problem lies not with the Rule's meaning but with the context in which it is applied. Police and judges operate in a finite zero-sum context. Their job is to end the game of "cops and robbers" with the cops catching the robbers, and the robbers going to jail, admittedly something that the police and judges would not want done to themselves. Criticizing the Golden Rule because it leads to the absurd—cops not catching robbers and judges not sentencing them—is as silly as criticizing basketball players for dribbling the ball down the court with their hands rather than kicking it down the court with their feet. The rules of basketball do not allow for kicking the ball, and if kicking the ball is what you want to do, then basketball is not the game you ought to be playing.

Similarly with regard to the Golden Rule: if your goal is to win at the expense of the other, then playing by the Golden Rule is going to lead to absurdities that will only frustrate you and cause you to criticize the Rule. But the problem isn't with the Golden Rule; it is with the game in which it is applied. Cops and robbers is a finite zero-sum game; the Golden Rule is for infinite nonzero games. Applying it to the former is no more rational than applying the rules of American soccer or European football to the game of basketball.

Recognizing this limitation to the applicability of the Golden Rule, the ethicist Robert Kurzman refers to the Golden Rule as "reciprocal altruism" and notes that "reciprocal altruism cannot emerge in organisms that do not interact repeatedly. More precisely, as the probability that one will encounter the same partner in the future decreases, the emergence of cooperation is less likely."[3]

According to Kurzman, the Golden Rule only works in cases where your interaction with someone is ongoing, a situation we are calling an infinite game. Indeed, while not explicitly using the language of finite and infinite games, Kurzman asserts that those who "defect" from the infinite to the finite game, that is, those who shift from nonzero interaction where all parties benefit to a zero-sum exchange where the "defector" wins at the expense of the others, are no longer operating in the realm of reciprocal altruism.[4]

Reciprocal altruism, or what I would call positive reciprocity, requires that person A give up some personal advantage in order to be of benefit to person B, with the expectation that person B will do the same regarding person A in the future.

Here is a simple and perhaps even commonplace example of positive reciprocity: Imagine you and a friend are having lunch, and as your friend takes out her wallet to pay for the meal, she unknowing drops a twenty-dollar bill on the floor. Picking up and pocketing the bill would be to your advantage, but instead you pick it up and return it to her, thus giving up personal advantage to be of benefit to your friend. The intrinsic understanding in this exchange is that your friend, if she is ever in a similar situation when it is you who has inadvertently dropped some cash, will do to you as you have done to her. This is a nonzero exchange—there is no winner or loser—in an infinite game of friendship, where the goal is to befriend one another in a manner that will perpetuate the friendship into the future. But is this the Golden Rule?

No, it isn't. The Golden Rule has no need of any intrinsic understanding of quid pro quo. Doing to others as you would want others to do to you will lead you to picking up and returning the dropped cash to your friend, but it will do so not because you are ensuring similar behavior on the part of the friend in the future, but because it is the right thing to do regardless of what may or may not happen in the future. Your only concern vis-à-vis the Golden Rule is perpetuating the relationship—the game, if you will—in the moment. If your friend reciprocates in the future, all the better, but that anticipated future is not the determining factor in choosing your action in the present. The Golden Rule is not synonymous with positive reciprocity.

It is commonplace to couch reciprocity in positive terms: returning kindness for kindness or trust with trust.

> Reciprocity is a moral virtue. We ought to be disposed, as a matter of moral obligation, to return good in proportion to the good we receive, and to make reparation for the harm we have done. Moreover, reciprocity is a fundamental virtue. Its requirements have presumptive priority over many competing considerations, and that priority

makes reciprocity a crucial consideration for a wide variety of important moral problems.[5]

Positive reciprocity, however, is not the only kind of reciprocity. The opposite of positive reciprocity is negative reciprocity. Negative reciprocity requires person A to give up some personal advantage to placate person B in hopes that in this way person B will not act in a manner that takes even more benefit from person A. This is a finite zero-sum exchange.

To see how this works, imagine an armed robber accosting you and demanding "your money or your life." Giving up your money in hopes that in this way you will get the robber to spare your life is a classic example of negative reciprocity. Clearly this is not the Golden Rule, and trying to apply the Golden Rule in this case would lead to more harm.

Doing to the robber as you would like the robber to do to you might lead you to ignore the robber—you certainly wish the robber had ignored you—and walk away, something you would like the robber to do as well. Chances are, however, that both ignoring the robber and walking away would simply escalate the situation, perhaps ending in your death.

Reciprocity can be both positive and negative, and neither is the same as the Golden Rule. You are being no less reciprocal when you return an insult with another insult, or a punch in the face with another punch in the face. In fact, the fundamental principle behind mutually assured destruction (MAD)—the military strategy that assumes the capacity of one nuclear state to reciprocate a nuclear first-strike attack with an equal or greater nuclear response, resulting in the mutually assured destruction of both attacker and attacked—is no less an example of reciprocity than an expression of the Golden Rule.

In the book of Exodus, for example, we find the following legal principle called *lex talionis*: "You shall give life for life, eye for eye, tooth for tooth, hand for hand, foot for foot, burn for burn, wound for wound, stripe for stripe" (Exodus 21:23–25). In the book of Leviticus we are told, "And if a person wounds another, he shall be so wounded in return: a break for a break, an eye for an eye, a tooth for a tooth; the wound he inflicts shall be inflicted upon him" (Leviticus 24:19–20). In the book of Deuteronomy judges are advised, "Show no pity: life for life, eye for eye, tooth for tooth, hand for hand, foot for foot" (Deuteronomy 19:21). These are laws rooted in the notion of reciprocity, but they are a far cry from the Golden Rule.

Reciprocity, as these examples show, is rooted in the notion of exchange: person A interacts with person B, and person B responds in kind. As ethicist Lawrence Becker notes:

> Social life is thick with exchanges—transactions that involve, for each party, both receipts and disbursements. Some of these exchanges are economic; others concern things that the parties are unwilling to treat as commodities. (Acts of love, for example.) For all of these exchanges, in all societies of record, there is apparently a norm of reciprocity, the form of which can be stated thus: Good is to be returned for good, but not necessarily for evil.[6]

This is why "the norm of reciprocity is not equivalent to the Golden Rule—found in Confucian, Talmudic, and Christian scriptural texts. That rule concerns more than exchanges, for one thing. It proposes a criterion for initiatives one might take: Do to others only what you would have them do to you."[7]

Although Becker is correct that the Golden Rule is concerned with more than exchanges, he is wrong to assume that this something more is the likes and dislikes of the person invoking the Rule. We have already seen that when applying the Golden Rule to the case of cops and robbers. Simply relying on your own preferences when defining actions condoned by the Golden Rule can lead to absurd results: police officers not arresting criminals, and judges not sentencing them. Something else has to be added to the formula, and that something else is the notion of infinite nonzero games: do to others what you would have them do to you if you are both seeking to maintain the relationship for the long term. In this context, the Golden Rule steps beyond reciprocity.

Jesus, for example, sometimes seems to reject reciprocity completely:

> You have heard that it was said, "An eye for an eye and a tooth for a tooth." But I say to you, Do not resist an evil-doer. But if anyone strikes you on the right cheek, turn the other also. (Matthew 5:38–39, NRSV)

> Love your enemies and pray for those who persecute you. (Matthew 5:44, NRSV)

> For if you love those who love you, what reward do you have? Do not even the tax collectors do the same? (Matthew 5:46, NRSV)

> Love your enemies, do good to those who hate you, bless those who curse you, pray for those who abuse you. (Luke 6:27–28, NRSV)

Reciprocity, the returning of one action with an equal action, in and of itself need not lead us to the Golden Rule:

> One who murders a fellow human shall be put to death. One who kills an animal shall pay a fine: life for life. One who maims a human will be maimed in like manner: shattered bone for shattered bone, lost eye for lost eye, broken tooth for broken tooth. That which was done to the other shall be done to the one. (Leviticus 24:17–20)

The Golden Rule, however, is not an in-kind response. In fact, the Golden Rule avoids reciprocity altogether:

> The issue is not just that you get what you send, that your karma might be back to bite you—you scratch my back and I'll scratch yours, and, if not, I'll scratch your eyes out. Rather, what is commanded rests on properly moral grounds: Each human self has real worth and dignity of just the sort that we would rightly claim in our own behalf. The command, then, is not mere bombast or hyperbole. It invites us to find worth in our own interest,

goals we cherish, values that build our personhood and give content to our claims to liberty. And, building on that foundation, it urges us to see and act on the recognition that others too have goals, needs, hopes, fears that matter *not just to them but objectively* in the same ways ours do. Love grounded in this way does not mean serving every caprice that might dart across another's fancy. Nor does it mean wanting for others just what we want for ourselves. Still less is it wanting others to be just like us.... The love that the Torah commends and commands means accepting the sanctity of each person's capacity to choose and cherish. We need not share each person's goals, and it's morally dubious to expect all human hopes to be alike. But our first obligation to one another is respect for subjecthood.[8]

Whether articulated in the positive or the negative, the Golden Rule does not rest on exchanges between people or on the quality of their actions in such an exchange. The Golden Rule rests solely on the preferences of the self. Neither "Do to others as you would want others to do to you" nor "Do not do to others what you would not want done to you" is linked to what the other person does or does not do. The Golden Rule is independent of the other's action or nonaction: Do to others what you would want others to do to you *regardless* of what others actually do to you. The ethical standard of the Golden Rule is not set by the other but by oneself. Hence, if we are going to understand how and why and in what context the Golden Rule operates, we had best be clear about what we mean by "self."

Who Am I?

The Golden Rule and the Nature of Self

As we noted in the previous chapter, the Golden Rule in all of its forms places the self at the heart of things: "Love your neighbor as yourself"; "Don't do to others what you would not want done to you"; "Do to others what you would want others to do to you." Doing so begs the question, who is this *you*? In this chapter we will attempt to answer this question in a manner that places the "self" in the context of infinite non-zero reality and in so doing makes the Golden Rule all the more golden.

What Is the Self upon Whom the Golden Rule Rests?

We opened chapter 1 with a 2,300-year-old insight from Aristotle. Here it is again in a slightly different translation:

> Humanity is by nature a social animal; an individual who
> is unsocial naturally and not accidentally is either beneath
> our notice or more than human. Society is something that
> precedes the individual. Anyone who either cannot lead
> the common life or is so self-sufficient as not to need to,

and therefore does not partake of society, is either a beast or a god.[1]

The self-in-society—your psychological self, your existential self—is the self that concerns us when investigating the Golden Rule. According to the psychologist Rollo May, the word "existence" enters the English language from the Latin root *existere*, "to stand out, emerge."[2] The existential self at the heart of the Golden Rule is this emerging self, the "I" that arises in the midst of life rather than an essentialist or cosmic "I" that is prior to that life. In this way, I am drawing on Jean Paul Sartre's notion that existence precedes essence:

> [Existence precedes essence means] that man first exists: he materializes in the world, encounters himself, and only afterward defines himself. If man as existentialists conceive of him cannot be defined, it is because to begin with he is nothing. He will not be anything until later, and then he will be what he makes of himself. Thus, there is no human nature since there is no God to conceive of it. Man is not only that which he conceives himself to be, but that which he wills himself to be, and since he conceives of himself only after he exists, just as he wills himself to be after being thrown into existence, man is nothing but what he makes of himself. This is the first principle of existentialism.... Man is nothing other than his own project. He exists only to the extent that he realizes himself, therefore he is nothing more than the sum of his actions, nothing more than his life.[3]

I find Sartre's position compelling, but I also find it a bit thin. While I agree that we are to a great degree what we make ourselves to be, this making doesn't happen in a vacuum. There are preexisting conditions—essences, if you like—into which we are born. These conditions determine just how much freedom we have with regard to our self-making. Race, gender, genetic predispositions, and class are but four major constraints that we have to work with. These constraints are givens and not the result of choices we make. May explains:

> For no matter how interesting or theoretically true is the
> fact that I am composed of such and such chemicals or
> act by such and such mechanisms or patterns, the cru-
> cial question always is that I happen to exist at this given
> moment in time and space, and my problem is how I am
> to be aware of that fact and what I shall do about it.[4]

So it is not a matter of existence versus essence but of how we shape
our existence given the preconditioned realities into which each of us is
born. With regard to the Golden Rule, one of the most important preexisting conditions is our reactive brain and the reptilian fight-or-flight
response it engenders. Working with this brain to overcome its essence
may be at the heart of what it is to be human: "For the living person ...
always transcends the given mechanism."[5] And the Golden Rule may be
among the greatest tools we have for doing so.

When talking about the nature of self, we are stepping into centuries of philosophical and scientific argument that has yet to come to any
generally agreed-upon conclusion. We will not pretend to accomplish
in these pages what great thinkers throughout history have failed to
accomplish in thousands of pages. Rather than prove that my understanding of self is the correct understanding of self, I will settle for
merely articulating what I understand the self to be in order to allow
you to draw your own conclusions. I take my understanding from the
work of American philosopher Daniel C. Dennett:

> A proper human self is the largely unwitting creation of
> an interpersonal design process in which we encourage
> small children to become communicators and, in particu-
> lar, to join our practice of asking for and giving reasons,
> and then reasoning about what to do and why. For this to
> work you have to start with the right raw materials. You
> won't succeed if you try it with your dog, for instance,
> or even a chimpanzee, as we know from a series of pro-
> tracted and enthusiastic attempts over the years. Some
> human infants are also unable to rise to the occasion. The
> first threshold on the path to personhood, then, is simply

whether or not one's caregivers succeed in kindling a communicator.[6]

From this first threshold the evolving self must tap into other talents: the talent to think, to reason, to control your behavior—all of which are influenced by both nature and nurture, two elements beyond your control. As Dennett says, "Not everybody can be a Shakespeare or a Bach, but almost everybody can learn to read and write well enough to become an informed citizen,"[7] assuming that the society in which you live allows for an informed citizenry—and that too may be beyond your control.

In the context of the Golden Rule, however, what matters is that the self can reason, that it can make decisions that have real impact on outcomes, and that it can communicate with others regarding why things are the way they are and how they might be made different than they are. Or, to be most specific, what matters is that the self can distinguish between finite and infinite games, analyze the benefits and drawbacks to each, and decide which games to play and which games not to play. Without this basic sense of self and agency there is no meaning or value to the Golden Rule at all. If you cannot choose which game to play and how to play it, choosing to play by the Golden Rule or any other rule is irrelevant.

I am prejudiced toward reason and the human capacity to think matters through in a rational way. But I also understand that reason doesn't operate in a vacuum. It is in fact influenced by irrational assumptions with which you are raised and in which you function. The free agency of self must be free to examine and test those assumptions and then change or abandon them for other assumptions over time. The Golden Rule is a rational rule to follow if the game you are playing is an infinite nonzero one. But that assumption and its opposite are assumptions that you have to test.

Selfish Gene

I have a friend named Gene. Yes, this is his real name, and I use it with his permission and with full knowledge of the pun it invokes. Gene and I have known each other for decades, and while we enjoy each other's company, we rarely accept each other's ideas. Gene is selfish, and unabashedly so. This bothers me. Not so much because of the way Gene acts but because the way he thinks is so damn difficult to refute.

According to Gene, life is one long but not infinite zero-sum game with very few winners and vast numbers of losers. While we all desire to be winners, Gene says, most of us will be losers. Winners are rare. They are the few who excel. They are the ones who can outrun, out-think, outwrestle, outshoot, and out-whatever everyone else.

As a species, we are winners. We have come, as the Hebrew Bible says we should, to dominate the entire planet (Genesis 1:28). While we may be fascinated by "Shark Week" on television, we need not fear an army of sharks rising up out the sea and threatening our survival. Sharks may take a bite out of some of us, but we can, and most likely will, do away with most if not all of them. We are so dominant on this planet that we have to invent alien species—killer robots from the future (*Terminator*), giant bugs from outer space (*Spaceship Troopers*), and autonomous and malevolent computer networks like those in *Tron* and *The Matrix*— just to give ourselves a good scare. But even then we write ourselves as the hero and make sure that in the end we humans still win.

Our selfishness is aimed not just at other species or space aliens; we turn on each other at the drop of a hat, a symbol, or an idea. It takes very little to get us warring and slaughtering one another. After all, what fun is it to win over whales? Sure, it was a challenge in Ahab's day, but Japanese whalers are not really at risk as they hunt these amazing mammals to extinction.

The real challenge, the best way to determine who among us are the true winners, is to dominate one another. So we set out to do just that. So obsessed are we with winning that we hope to dominate others not only in this life but in the life to come as well. We want to be winners in this world and the next.

Armies are the way we secure our alpha status in this world. Religion is the way we do it in the world to come. This is why armies and religions often go hand in hand. We conquer, kill, or convert "the other" in this world because our God—the God of our imagination— insists on it. Not yet satisfied, we imagine those who continue to resist us will suffer eternal torment and torture at the hands of our imagined God as well. True, this is more easily seen in the three major Abrahamic faiths—Judaism, Christianity, and Islam—but, as we have seen, Hinduism and Buddhism are not exempt from sanctifying war and promoting karmically sanctioned zero-sum societies plagued by caste and misogyny.

We invent all of this because we want to win, and we define winning in a zero-sum way: I win only if you lose. Because I want to win in this world, I act in ways that see that you do not win. Because I want to win in the next world, I imagine you burning in hellfire while I bask in the cool graces of some heavenly realm or Buddhaland.

All of this makes perfect sense to my friend Gene. This is Gene's worldview. Humans are selfish. Everything we do, everything we invent, everything we believe in revolves around our passion for winning. Our passion for winning is fueled by our delight in other people losing. Gene loves quoting from the great Catholic theologian Saint Thomas Aquinas:

> Nothing should be denied the blessed that belongs to the perfection of their beatitude.... Wherefore in order that the happiness of the saints may be more delightful to them and that they may render more copious thanks to God for it, they are allowed to see perfectly the sufferings of the damned.[8]

Gene quotes Aquinas with relish: "Are you following what he is saying? The saved are all the more happy when they get to watch the torment of the damned! Can you see how perverse that is? And this is from a man who is supposed to be a religious genius. Maybe he is, I don't know, but if he is, I can be pretty certain that his religion is madness."

Is Gene wrong?

The Game of Black-and-White

I've heard Gene argue against some pretty sophisticated minds, and I have never seen him toppled. "Are you saying, Gene, that there is no cooperation in nature?" "Of course not," Gene would say. "Who can deny the symbiotic relationships between bees and flowers, for example, or the level of cooperation in which people engage?

"When I go to the supermarket to purchase milk, I rely on dairy farmers to care for and milk the cows, truck drivers to get the milk to market, white-collar executives to run the markets, blue-collar workers to stock the shelves and run the cash registers. But none of this is done for me. People are simply acting in their own self-interest, and I benefit from it. This is how selfishness promotes survival for the winners. But it is no less selfish for doing so."

I see things very differently. Life as I see it is what Zen teacher Alan Watts called the Game of Black-and-White. Life as Gene sees it is the Game of Black-or-White.[9] In the Game of Black-and-White, white is defined only in relation to black, and black is defined only in relation to white. These seeming opposites are in fact complementarities. They go together like front and back, up and down, in and out. Front exists only in relation to back, up makes sense only in relation to down, and "in" can be "in" only when our thinking includes "out."

Many years ago, I sought to teach the Game of Black-and-White to a class of sixth graders in Taos, New Mexico. I took the class outside to gaze at the surrounding mountains. They were used to it, but I was living in Miami, Florida, at the time, and these mountain peaks were breathtaking to me.

"I love the majesty of these mountains," I told the class. "But, honestly, the valleys are boring. Wouldn't it be cool if we could fill in the valleys and just have only peaks?"

The kids looked at one another as if to ask, "Is he serious?" I went on about this idea a bit more to make it clear that I would really love to fill in the valleys in favor of more mountains.

"But if you did that," one girl said in a dismissive tone, "we wouldn't have any mountains at all, only flat ground. Everything would be equal. We need the valleys to have the mountains."

I sat with that thought for a moment, and then said, "And we need the mountains to have the valleys?"

"Of course," several children said at once.

"Then why do we call them mountains and valleys? If they each need the other, why don't we call them mountain-valleys or valley-mountains?"

This started everyone laughing, and we entered into a solid discussion of how everything goes with everything else and, if you want one thing, everything else is going to come along with it.

"Including good and bad?" one girl asked.

"Yes, including good and bad."

"So we should really talk about 'good-bad' rather than 'good and bad,'" another student said. I agreed.

"Then why be good at all?'

It is one thing to recognize that opposites like good and bad are complements; it is another to then say that because good and bad go together, doing good and doing bad are morally equivalent. They are not.

There are two basic answers to the question "Why do good?": You do good to win a reward, either in this life or the next; or you do good because doing good perpetuates something greater than yourself.

My friend Selfish Gene would snicker at this point and say, "I told you so! It's always about you." And it is. Where Gene and I disagree is over just what this "you" is, how it functions, and what is in its best interest.

All forms of the Golden Rule are, well, rules—commands: do this or don't do that. The assumption of all such commands is that there is both a commander and a commanded. Both assumptions are problematic.

Who Am I?

Often when we talk about the Golden Rule there is a sense that it comes from God, but this is only a cultural bias. Although it is true that the God YHVH commands the Jews to "love your neighbor as yourself," and the Christian God Jesus commands his followers to "do to others as you would have them do to you," Confucius, perhaps the first to articulate the Golden Rule, speaks only from his own authority, and Hillel, in reducing all of God's Torah to "what is hateful to you do not do to another" is not quoting from the Hebrew Bible but relying only on his own understanding of it.

Who Am I? 77

The command can come from a god, a sage, or one's own reasoning, so a divine Commander may not be necessary. But what is the necessity of there being someone to command, someone who can choose to follow the command or not? Does the Golden Rule make any sense if there is no free agent to be commanded?

Commanding someone to do "x" only makes sense if that someone is capable of deciding to do "y" when "y" equals "not-x." In other words, commanding me to love my neighbor only makes sense if I can choose not to love my neighbor. Choice is essential to the equation.

If choosing to love my neighbor is to be a meaningful choice, I have to be free to hate my neighbor as well. My experience, however, suggests that choosing to love or hate is not something I freely do at all. Love and hate are emotions that "happen" to me, not choices I make from a neutral deliberative stance. I don't meet people and then make a conscious choice to love or hate them. Most people leave me emotionally neutral: I have no strong attraction or repulsion with regard to them. In fact, it would be a very difficult life if we lived with strong emotions regarding everyone we met.

Given my immediate neutrality toward someone, we might say I can choose to love or to hate as I will, but is it really a matter of choice? If I find myself loving or hating someone, it is rarely, if ever, a matter of choice. I don't choose to feel one way or another; I simply notice that I feel one way or another. So if "I" am not making a choice, who is?

The question is far from settled.

Being of Two Minds and a Body

Although it feels to us that we have free will, that there is a "me" that decides just what it is "I" will think, feel, and do, scientific investigation into this "me" leaves things far more muddied than my subjective sense of self would allow.

The human brain has two hemispheres connected by the corpus callosum. The purpose of the corpus callosum is to allow each hemisphere to communicate with the other so that they might collaborate in decision making. While we are rarely aware of these two hemispheres and do not think of ourselves as being of two minds, split-brain experiments suggest otherwise.

People suffering from a damaged corpus callosum often find themselves with two brains no longer in communication with one another. The result can be most striking.

Michael Gazzaniga is among the leading scientists doing split-brain studies. In one experiment, he showed each hemisphere of a split-brain patient a different picture. The right hemisphere (through the left eye) was shown a picture of snow; the left hemisphere (through the right eye) was shown a picture of a chicken's foot. He then showed a series of pictures to both hemispheres and asked the patient to choose which among the series of pictures went with the picture originally shown.

The patient's left hand pointed to a shovel corresponding to the picture of snow it was shown. The patient's right hand pointed to a picture of a chicken corresponding to the picture of a chicken's foot it was shown. This makes perfect sense because the right hemisphere of the brain controls the left side of the body, while the left hemisphere of the brain controls the right side. When asked to explain the choice, the patient spoke only to the chicken's foot/chicken pair of pictures, ignoring the snow/shovel pair entirely. This, too, makes sense because verbal skills are controlled by the left hemisphere of the brain, the hemisphere that was shown the chicken's foot picture.

Gazzaniga then drew the patient's attention to the choice of the shovel made by his left hand/right hemisphere. When asked to explain why his left hand chose the shovel, the patient explained that the shovel was needed to clean out the chicken coop. The point here isn't that the right hemisphere is irrational; it clearly isn't. The point is that lacking complete information (in this case, the left hemisphere lacking any knowledge of the picture of snow shown to the right hemisphere), the brain will fabricate a story to make sense of the choice it has already made.

The real reason the patient chose the shovel was because his right hemisphere was shown a picture of snow, but this fact was lost to him. Rather than say, "I don't know why I chose a shovel in response to a chicken's foot," the patient invented a reason rather than admit ignorance.[10]

Could this preference for fabrication in the face of ignorance speak to the larger issue of free will and agency? According to current scientific research, our brains decide to initiate action $\frac{1}{32}$ of a second prior to our conscious minds becoming aware of that action. As inventor and futurist Ray Kurzweil puts it, "We are apparently very eager to explain and rationalize our actions, even when we didn't actually make the decisions that led to them."[11]

So is there a "me" or not? Neuroscientist V. S. Ramachandran introduces the problem this way:

> Sometime in the twenty-first century science will confront one of its last great mysteries: the nature of self.... The search for self—and the solutions to its many mysteries—is hardly a new pursuit. This area of study has traditionally been the preserve of philosophers, and it is fair to say that on the whole they haven't made a lot of progress.... Nevertheless, philosophy has been extremely useful in maintaining semantic hygiene and emphasizing the need for clarity in terminology.[12]

Ramachandran focuses on two terms used in the study of consciousness: *qualia*, the sensations experienced by the body; and *self*, that aspect of consciousness that knows it is experiencing qualia. For example, when I look at a red wagon, the quality of redness is qualia; my knowing I am seeing a red wagon is self. Ramachandran sees qualia and self as different from one another, even as he acknowledges that they cannot be separated from one another: there are no qualities to experience if there is no experiencer to experience them.[13]

According to Ramachandran, the self is a relatively small cluster of brain areas that are linked into an amazingly powerful network. This cluster gives rise to a sense of self that has seven characteristics:

1. Unity: Outwardly you are bombarded by an enormous amount of diverse experiences, and inwardly you contain a wide spectrum of hopes, dreams, goals, values, memories, feelings, and the like. You nevertheless feel like a single person.

2. Continuity: Although you change physically, emotionally, intellectually, and spiritually over time, you nevertheless identify the "you" at your birth with the "you" of your childhood, adolescence, and adulthood. When you see a photograph of yourself taken decades ago, you immediately identify that self as "me" even though there may be little in common between that younger self and the self you are today.

3. Embodiment: You identify your physical body with your self, even though that body is changing.

4. Privacy: Your thoughts, feelings, and sensations take place inside your brain where others cannot observe them.

5. Social embedding: We are so tightly linked to the world around us that we attribute agency to events that may be merely accidents, and motives to people who may have acted without any forethought. If your computer freezes, for example, you may become angry at it, as if it were making a choice, when in fact it is not conscious at all. Ramachandran sees this aspect of self as central to the creation of religion: we attribute agency to accidents and invent gods who control such events and who can be convinced to control to our benefit through acts of worship and sacrifice.

6. Free will: True or not, we see our selves as free agents rather than conditioned robots forced to operate one way or another based on programs over which we have no control.

7. Self-awareness: The self has the capacity to observe itself and to realize the previous six attributes unique to the self. It is this element of selfhood that most of us take to be the key attribute of ourselves.[14]

Where Am I?

Although I am grateful to Ramachandran for his careful dissection of self, I wonder whether he has actually uncovered a self. Is there a "me" inside my body or brain that can be represented by a dot on a map with the caption "You Are Here"?

The answer is no. There is no self distinct from the activity of the brain, and since the activity of the brain is part of the activity of the body, and the activity of the body is part of the activity of the environment that sustains that body, the self is simply—and wondrously—an expression of the activity of the universe. The universe "selfs" the way an apple tree "apples."

There are some people who will take this notion of the absence of a separate and sovereign self as proof that there is no free will and therefore no morality. You cannot be responsible for your actions if there is no one directing those actions. But is that what Ramachandran is telling us? Is there really "no one home"?

My answer to this question is calculated: it depends. If we are looking for a self that can be separated from the seven attributes outlined by Ramachandran, I think the answer is no, there is no such self. Even if there were such a self, of what value would it be to us? The self that matters to us is the self that we imagine is continuous with the various stages of our growth and experiences of our lives. If the self is other than the me I take myself to be when I look at photographs of myself old and new; if the self is other than the me that has "my parents," "my spouse," "my children," then the self isn't really me at all. If it is this self that exercises free agency over me, then it is that self and not me that is responsible for what I do.

If, however, I take a more humble view of self, focusing on Ramachandran's seventh attribute, self-awareness, then I clearly have a self. Indeed I am that self. As a self-aware being I can see clearly that much of what I do, I do unconsciously. I don't direct my heart to beat or my neurons to fire. They simply operate via instructions with which I have nothing to do. I don't control the thoughts and feelings that arise into my field of awareness. I can't make myself angry or loving, or stop myself from feeling anger or love when these arise from conditions over which I have no control.

What I can do is process the data that arise in my conscious awareness. I can notice feelings of anger and choose to act on them or not. I can notice feelings of love and choose to act on them or not. I can't control all my behavior—indeed I would die if I had to consciously beat my heart or oxygenate my blood—but I can control enough of it to promote relationships between myself and others that are either zero-sum or nonzero sum. This is the only self I care about.

The Self and the Golden Rule

Now what does this tell us about the Golden Rule? Plenty. Remember, the Golden Rule, unlike reciprocity, does not depend on the actual exchange you have with another being. Reciprocity tells us to reciprocate kindness with kindness but not to reciprocate cruelty with kindness. The Golden Rule, on the other hand, takes matters outside any specific exchange and says that regardless of what others do to you, do kindly to them because that is what you want them to do to you.

This is taking self-awareness to a higher level and liberating ethical standards from any given exchange. The Golden Rule, unlike reciprocity, is not a matter of situational ethics, but an a priori position taken by a self-aware mind that is committed to something greater than the situation at hand. What is that something greater? Infinite nonzero play.

Think of a relationship with a loved one. Although there will be situations in which the other acts in needlessly hurtful ways toward you, your commitment to infinite play urges you not to respond to the facts on the ground but to the ideals in the mind—Ramachandran's seventh attribute, self-awareness. Rather than reciprocating via the reptilian brain and its fight-or-flight response, either of which will end the game with one of you being the winner and the other the loser, you act toward the other in a manner that will maintain the game, and this, as Jesus taught, often calls us to love our enemies (Matthew 5:44).

Why Is the Golden Rule Ubiquitous?

People are often amazed at the ubiquity of the Golden Rule. Why is it that across human history and culture we find both the theory and the practice of the Golden Rule?

According to evolutionary psychologists, the answer is that the Golden Rule occurs among species whose survival depends on the survival of the group or community: "Among animals species and humans who live in groups, being in the group apparently provides advantages for survival and the raising of young: shared resources, divisions of labor, mutual defense, and so forth."[15]

Natural selection is biased toward individuals in a group who promote group survival and hence promote the survival of the Golden Rule gene over the selfish gene. Playing well with others has an evolutionary advantage, or as American biologist Edward O. Wilson puts it, "Compassion is selective and often ultimately self-serving."[16]

In addition to natural selection, social cohesion plays a role. Although nature selects for compassion, communities themselves promote compassion by welcoming the team player and alienating the less cooperative. Our brains, according to neuroscientist Donald Pfaff, "are excellent at detecting cheaters who are breaking a social contract. Moreover, we come equipped with a sense of moral outrage. Thus, with both our highly developed cognitive capacities and our strong emotional dispositions, we are ready to impose sanctions on those who deviate from reciprocal altruism."[17]

But, as we have seen, the Golden Rule is not the same as reciprocal altruism. Neither "Do to others as you would have them do to you" nor "What is hateful to you do not do to others" implies reciprocity. A reciprocal rule would say, "Do to others as you would have them do to you only when they do to you as you would have them or only when their doing so is a near certainty."

The Golden Rule's reference to self serves only to help you judge the quality of your action; the action itself is selfless. Let's look at this carefully: Doing or not doing to others is the Rule. What you do or refrain from doing, the quality of what you do, is linked to yourself. The Rule requires you to do something you think another will like, based on your own experience, or not do something to another that you think the other will not like, again based on your experience. There is nothing reciprocal about this at all. Even if you know that others will not do to you, or even if you know that what they will do to you, based on their experience, is not something you even want done, you are still obligated to do to them as you would have them do to you.

This is true because as evolutionarily beneficial the Golden Rule may be to both individual and group survival, the Rule itself is something more, something revolutionary as well. Although the cultivating of reciprocal altruism is good in and of itself, it doesn't shift us from zero-sum to nonzero thinking or from finite to infinite gaming. Only the Golden Rule does this.

Shifting Games

There is, however, insight derived from the scientific study of reciprocal altruism that is applicable to the Golden Rule. As neuroscientist Donald Pfaff puts it, "We are more likely to treat another person properly if we expect to see that person again and again. We will obey this rule if we sense that we inhabit the same 'space,' the same social domain as the other person. The two of us feel subject to shared fates; we don't harm people with whom we share fates."[18]

This is true in both finite and infinite play and in both zero-sum and nonzero worldviews. The difference is this: In the finite zero-sum world, there are shared spaces and unshared spaces, and there are people with whom we share these spaces and people with whom we share no space at all. In the infinite nonzero world, all space is shared space, and all beings are beings with whom we share this space. In the finite world we share fate with some; in the infinite world we share fate with all.

I am arguing that the Golden Rule functions only in shared space and with the people, animals, and things with which we share that space. There is no need for the Golden Rule if we are as Aristotle's beasts or gods, living in isolation in unshared space. I am further arguing that the more we understand the nature of self and the fact that this self is a function not simply of one's brain but also of the universe as a whole, the more we realize that all space is shared space and that we share this space with all beings, human and otherwise.

This realization makes the Golden Rule the ultimate guide for right living. Or conversely, working with the Golden Rule shifts our worldview from the finite zero-sum world of isolated self and limited shared space to the infinite nonzero world of absolute shared space and, as Thich Nhat Hanh put it in chapter 3, inter-are, or inter-being.

Even if you agree with me that the Golden Rule functions optimally in the world of infinite nonzero exchange, we are still left with the question, why does it function at all?

According to Pfaff, the key mechanisms behind the Golden Rule are fear and the loss of information. His theory has four steps. The following is adapted from his book *The Neuroscience of Fair Play: Why We (Usually) Follow the Golden Rule.* Imagine the following:

Step One: Ms. A fantasizes about murdering Mr. B with repeated stab wounds to his stomach.

Step Two: Ms. A imagines Mr. B. with multiple stab wounds.

Step Three: Ms. A "blurs the difference" between Mr. B and herself, seeing herself as the victim of a stabbing rather than Mr. B, her intended victim.

Step Four: Ms. A is less likely to carry out her attack, fearing in herself what Mr. B would fear in himself should the attack occur, and recoiling from it.[19]

This is the negative articulation of the Golden Rule: what is hateful to you—in this case, being stabbed—do not do to another. For the neuroscientists, this explanation of an ethical decision by the would-be killer has one very attractive feature: it involves only the loss of information, not its effortful acquisition or storage.

The learning of complex information and its storage in memory are deliberate, painstaking processes, but the *loss* of information seems to take place with no trouble at all. Damping any of the many mechanisms involved in memory can explain the blurring of identity required by this theory.... The attacker temporarily puts herself in the other person's place. She avoids an unethical act because of shared fear.[20]

Pfaff's notion of blurring identities finds expression in the Hebrew Bible: "Love your neighbor as yourself" (Leviticus 19:18) and "Love the stranger as yourself" (Leviticus 19:34). His neuroscientific approach to these ideas provides us with insight into how they can actually be accomplished.

The blurring, he says, takes place in the cerebral cortex, where clusters of cells responsible for self-identity can be turned on or turned off. One way to turn off the self-identifiers is through excitation. The mechanisms of excitation and the brain chemistry involved are of little importance to our study. What matters here is simply the fact that you can, by exciting certain cells in the brain, lose your capacity to separate yourself from others, and in so doing come to see your neighbor as yourself.

Golden Hormones

According to Pfaff, there is evidence that there is "an ethical switch" residing in the prefrontal cortex or the amygdala that, when stimulated, blurs the distinction of self and other, revealing the neighbor and the stranger as "myself." "The result is empathic behavior that obeys the Golden Rule."[21] Pfaff says:

> All forms of social bonding appear to stem from the same wellspring of the most basic human relationships. "I love him like a brother!" "She's been like a daughter to me all these years." We all have heard these expressions, which speak volumes about the biological reference point of our varied social connections. If, as I propose, loving, supportive relations typical of stable sex partners and families blend into our feelings for friends and acquaintances in general, then the mechanisms of sexual and parental behaviors ... should be able to tell us a great deal about mechanisms for the friendly, ethical behaviors that conform to the Golden Rule.[22]

In other words, Pfaff suggests, there are Golden Rule hormones. Chief among these is oxytocin, a hormone produced by the hypothalamus that is responsible for friendly, ethical behaviors. Oxytocin is the motherhood hormone. When the amount of oxytocin is increased, the levels of maternal feelings and behaviors are increased. When the amount of oxytocin is blocked and decreased, there is a corresponding decrease in maternal instinct. One of the ways—and for our purposes, the most important way—oxytocin achieves what it does is by lowering the level of fear and anxiety.

Although oxytocin research often involves aspects of motherhood, the hormone itself is not "female." Both women and men have oxytocin receptors in their brains and spinal cords. In all humans, oxytocin functions to reduce fear and increase trust. This association with trust is what may make oxytocin a prime candidate for the Golden Rule hormone. (Another hormone, vasopressin, seems to act similarly, and researchers suggest that both oxytocin and vasopressin evolved from a common hormone called vasotocin.)

In a brain-imaging study conducted by Andreas Meyer-Lindenberg at the National Institute for Mental Health, volunteers viewed violent and frightening images strong enough to excite the amygdala, the part of the brain we might call "fear central." Volunteers were given oxytocin or a placebo by nasal spray. Those who got the hormone responded less fearfully than those who got the placebo. Brain images showed that the hormone blocked or dampened the impact of the images on the amygdala, which is why, we assume, their level of fear was less.[23]

To Spray or Not to Spray?

Given the data, and what I have mentioned here is but a mere smattering of it, would we be wise to equip ourselves with oxytocin nasal sprays to inhibit fear and promote social cohesion and the Golden Rule? It might not be that simple, but it is a thought experiment worth pursuing.

What if we could market a safe and effective spray that would work with our brain chemistry to make us more open to a nonzero worldview and infinite play? Does the Golden Rule have to be something we willfully adopt, or can it be hardwired into us via chemical adjustments?

The answers to these questions lead us back to finite and infinite games. If you believe that you are an isolated individual seeking to optimize your success (however defined) by your own efforts—in other words, if you play a finite zero-sum game—then you will likely reject the use of a drug to make you a better person. If, on the other hand, you see yourself as part of a single bio-system and your goal is to optimize the success of the entire system rather than just yourself—in other words, if you play an infinite nonzero game—then you will be more likely to say yes to a Golden Rule spray. Indeed, you might, in the interests of doing to others, seek to mandate such chemical intervention by law.

Remember, the Golden Rule isn't "live and let live" but, regardless of the actions of the other, behave toward the other in a manner that will benefit the other. Wouldn't it be beneficial for all humans to decrease their levels of anxiety and increase their capacity for love and social connection?

You've Got a Friend

Lucky for us there is more to the neuroscience of the Golden Rule than oxytocin. The key to the neuroscience of the Golden Rule may be the blurring of identities—loving neighbor and stranger as yourself—but oxytocin is not all there is to it.

> What actually takes place when people (or animals, for that matter) form a new social bond or strike a new friendship? First, we must learn the other's identity so that we can remember and recognize it. Second, assuming that the other person has not harmed us—no danger there—we recognize him or her as a friend. Then we can blur that person's features, his or her identity, with our own. We can "love that person as ourselves."[24]

How does this happen? Not surprisingly, recognition takes place in the amygdala and is linked to increased levels of oxytocin. Friendship, too, seems to be the amygdala's bailiwick. "Note how the amygdala keeps emerging as a brain structure that is key to upholding the Golden Rule!"[25]

According to social scientist James Q. Wilson, reciprocity is universal. "If we do a favor, we expect one in return. If we receive a favor we cannot return, we are distressed."[26] Wilson takes his argument from the mechanisms of parental care to the basic human desire for attachment—a friendly social environment fostered by ethical, fair, sympathetic behavior.

But again, this is not the Golden Rule. This is reciprocity. I cannot stress enough that the two are not the same and yet are constantly equated nonetheless. Neuroscientist Donald Pfaff, for all his excellent study of the brain and the Golden Rule, never seems to make the distinction. When commenting on how easy it is for us to break the Golden Rule, a fact we have documented several times in this book, Pfaff offers us the following:

> How can the Golden Rule be trumped so readily? Surprisingly enough, committing a scandalous act does not always mean throwing out the Golden Rule. For example, one form of illegality, not warlike or violent, has peculiar relation to the ethical principle I have been discussing. From New York to Moscow to Macao, we hear about corruption: people getting favors from officials in return for illegal compensation. Why should this happen? The answer might appear shocking. Corruption, which seems to be just as universal as the observance of the Golden Rule, is nothing less but its extension—outside the law. "You do something for me; I do something for you." With the corrupt duo, it is a form of reciprocal altruism, albeit illegal.[27]

But as I have been arguing throughout this book, the Golden Rule is not about reciprocity. It is engaging the other in a manner that is beneficial to the other whether or not the other reciprocates and does something beneficial to you. Corruption takes place only in a finite zero-sum game. The goal of corruption is to get something at the expense of others—that is, to win while others lose. This has nothing to do with the Golden Rule, and confusing reciprocity with the Rule blurs the necessary distinction between finite and infinite games and zero-sum and nonzero worldviews essential to understanding the Golden Rule.

Let Them Eat Cake. But How Much?

Evolutionary theorist Brian Skyrms introduces what he calls the cake-splitting game in his book *Evolution of the Social Contract*.[28] Here is the game as simply as I can put it: Two people are asked by a referee to split a cake between them. If the percentages of the cake each person requests total more than 100 percent (if, for example, each person desires 66 percent of the cake), neither person gets any cake. If the total is less than 100 percent, each person gets the amount requested. As Skyrms notes, the most stable strategy, the one that will keep the peace between the players, is for each person to ask for half the cake.

A less than optimal solution, but one that would continue to promote peace between the players, is if one player requests one-third of the cake and the other asks for two-thirds. While not an equal division, this is still a fair solution, since each person gets what is requested. But what if each player demands the entire cake?

According to the rules, since the total percentage of cake demanded would exceed 100 percent, no one would get any cake. Knowing this, the rational player, using Ramachandran's seventh characteristic of self, self-awareness, would request no more than half a cake.

Even a cursory look at the conflicts threatening human life and the natural world around the globe would make clear that we humans don't always operate from this seventh characteristic. All too often we seek to grab the whole cake without taking long-term consequences seriously at all. It just isn't all that clear to us that if we all strive to have it all, we will find ourselves with nothing at all.

In other words, finite zero-sum games are a lower level of self-functioning than infinite nonzero games. What makes the latter a higher functioning of self is the self's capacity to consider the long-term consequences of its actions. True, as my friend Gene might point out, the consideration is still self-focused, but the self in this case is aware of its inter-being with all other selves and hence knows that its long-term success depends on the long-term success of all other beings as well. Again, the Golden Rule elevates the level of exchange from finite to infinite and from zero-sum to nonzero.

Given all of this, let me add an element to Ramachandran's seventh characteristic of self: the capacity of self-awareness to determine the quality of play, choosing between finite zero-sum games and infinite nonzero games. Whether such a self exists independent of the body and the biosphere that manifests the body is irrelevant because the primary function of the self is to optimize one's success in the incarnate world of interdependent bodies and beings. A self who views the world as a zero-sum game will follow a finite strategy, seeking to starve others of cake. A self who views the world as a nonzero game will follow an infinite strategy that shares the cake in order to maintain the optimal quality of play.

In the context of the Golden Rule, this is the only self that matters and the only free agency that is necessary, because the Golden Rule is only golden in the context of infinite nonzero play.

Cake in the Kingdom

There is one last element to Skyrms's cake game that is relevant here. The game assumes a finite cake. That is what the referee is there to enforce. If the sum total of cake requested by the players exceeds 100 percent of the cake, the referee deprives both players of cake. But what if the referee's job were changed? What if in the case of each player demanding 100 percent of the cake, the referee bakes another cake?

This would be a truly nonzero game. This is the game Jesus envisions as the kingdom of God. Of all the miracles recorded in the Christian scriptures, only two appear in all four Gospels: the resurrection of Jesus and the feeding of five thousand men (the women and children present are fed but not counted) with five loaves and two fishes (Matthew 14:13–21; Mark 6:30–44; Luke 9:10–17; John 6:1–15). A similar miracle involving four thousand men, seven loaves of bread, and a "few small fish" occurs in Mark and Matthew (Mark 8:1–9; Matthew 15:32–39).

In Jesus's hands what would certainly have been a finite and insufficient amount of food manages to feed a multitude. The world Jesus envisions isn't a finite world of scarce resources but an infinite world where there is enough for everyone. This is not Skyrms's game. There is no referee in Jesus's world, and players are not pitted against one another. There is simply enough for everyone; no one loses.

John's telling of the story is especially nonzero. According to John, Jesus instructs his disciples to give the people as much as they want (John 6:11). After the feast he has them collect whatever is left over. By John's reckoning the leftovers total twelve full baskets of bread (John 6:13). In Jesus's world, unlike Skyrms's world, there is no shortage of cake, and because there is no shortage of cake, there is no need for referees. Everybody gets everything.

The question we must ask is this: which world do we live in?

Tea, Earl Grey, Hot

Fans of *Star Trek: The Next Generation* are most likely familiar with the preferred beverage of Jean-Luc Picard, captain of the USS *Enterprise*: "tea, Earl Grey, hot." We know this because when he desires a cup of hot Earl Grey tea he speaks to the computer that runs his replicator and says, "Tea. Earl Grey. Hot." And the machine makes him a cup of tea by assembling atoms in such a manner as to produce an authentic cup of hot Earl Grey tea. Since atoms are for all practical purposes infinite in number, the replicator can produce an infinite amount of nonliving things. (Replicators cannot create antimatter, dilithium, latinum, or any type of living being. Even twenty-fourth-century technology has its limits.)

I raise the issue of the replicator in the sci-fi world of *Star Trek* to make the following point: Although the technology is such that one can replicate whatever one desires, thus rendering obsolete the scarcity of most goods, the various species in the *Star Trek* universe are often at war. Why? The *Star Trek* universe could be totally nonzero. No one need go hungry, naked, or homeless. Energy, with the exception of dilithium, seems to be renewable, so what are they fighting about?

The answer is simple: they fight over the three things the replicator cannot produce: latinum, dilithium, and power—usually power over other species or planets. In other words, they—and we—fight over the things that are scarce. We fight over Dr. Skyrms's cake.

Scarcity and the fear of not having enough of whatever scarce commodity we deem to be of value seem to be major motivators of human activity. They are what get our games in play. But games based on scarcity are finite zero-sum games.

It may well be that we are evolutionarily programmed to play such games, but it also seems to be true that we can change the game from zero-sum to nonzero and that doing so is the role of the self (or at least the seventh characteristic of the self) guided by the Golden Rule.

Natural selection has shaped much of our decision making; we have agency, but it is not all that free. But natural selection goes only so far. Human beings live in a secondary world of culture, a world of our own creation. This world runs on memes rather than genes, and the source of memes—elements of culture that we use to define our reality and make rational decisions based on that definition—is us.

If we are driven by the meme of zero-sum scarcity, then we are driven to play a finite game in which we seek to gain control over the scarce resources we desire at the expense of others who seek to do the same. If we are driven by the meme of nonzero abundance, then we are driven to play an infinite game in which the goal is to create Jesus's kingdom of God, a world of abundance where no one need dominate anyone else.

> We can conceive (we think) of better worlds and yearn to get there.... Our evolved capacity to reflect gives us— and only us—both the opportunity and the competence to evaluate the ends, not just the means. We have to use our current values as the starting point for any contemplated revaluation of values, but from our perspective on our current hilltop, we can formulate, criticize, revise, and—if we are lucky—mutually endorse a set of design principles for living in society.[29]

The Golden Rule is one of these memes, and the one that may well be best suited for moving us from zero-sum scarcity and the finite games that pit people against people, and people against the planet, toward nonzero abundance and the infinite game of Jesus's kingdom of God. The question still to be answered is this: are we free to use the meme to shift our sense of reality and thus come to see the Golden Rule as the optimal guide to playing well? We will tackle this question in the next chapter.

To Do or Not to Do

The Golden Rule and Free Agency

"Do to others" or "Don't do to others"—the assumption is the same: it is your choice. But is it? Are you a free agent with free will capable of doing or not doing as you choose? In the previous chapter we looked at the nature of the self and how it might work with the Golden Rule. In this chapter we will focus on one aspect of this self: moral free agency.

Chances are you are by now aware of the three primary shapers of decision making: nature, nurture, and social pressure. It comes as no surprise to you that you were born with certain genetic preferences, causing your brain to lean one way or another when it comes to making choices. It is probably no less shocking to learn that your history, your experiences as a child, and the way you were raised also push you in one direction or another when it comes to matters of moral choice. And it doesn't take but a moment and a bit of self-observation to notice the pressure peers and social groups place upon you when it comes to making choices, moral and otherwise. Yet if you are like most of us, you nonetheless assume there is a part of you—the most important part of you perhaps—that can sidestep these forces and make your own decisions for your own reasons. You presume to have—irrespective of biology, history, and society—free will. You assume, despite everything you have just read about neuroscience and the nature of self in the previous chapter, that you are a free agent—your choices are your own and you are responsible for them.

As strong as this presumed feeling of free agency may be, however, there is plenty of evidence suggesting this feeling is not indicative of a universal truth, but is merely a cultural narrative arising from Judaism, Christianity, and Islam and embedded in Western civilization.

The Golden Rule as Game Changer

I'm not claiming that you make no choices, only that your choosing is done in a larger context than that of some hypothetical "free agent." Morals arises in situ, and as I have been arguing throughout this book, there are two basic categories of situation: zero-sum and nonzero. There is a moral preference associated with each category, and the Golden Rule is the preferred guide in nonzero situations only. It is not a matter of willing yourself into following the Rule, something that is rarely successful. Rather, it is a matter of understanding which situation you are in and acting accordingly. When you are playing a finite zero-sum game, play by the rules of finite zero-sum gaming: win by all means necessary. Or, if this bothers you because of the long-term consequences, don't seek to impose the Golden Rule on a finite game, but shift the game to infinite nonzero play and allow the Golden Rule to function naturally of its own accord.

In other words, it may be the case that you cannot willfully impose the Golden Rule on finite zero-sum situations, and there is no need to impose it on infinite nonzero ones. Don't change the rules; change the game. This is the argument I have been presenting throughout this book. I am restating it only to set up our discussion of free agency. So let's go back to the notion of free agent, a "you" that is unencumbered by the forces of biology, history, and society; a psychological "you" independent of the brain.

The Ladder of Moral Development

Because this "you" is a psychological phenomenon, it is only natural that we turn to psychologists to help us understand how it develops morally. Chief among these psychologists is Lawrence Kohlberg, whose notion that humans move gradually through six stages of moral development has dominated the field since the 1960s.

Here are the six stages as simply as I can put them:

- Stage one: Right and wrong are determined by those with the power to reward or punish me, and my actions are based on my desire to earn the former and avoid the latter.
- Stage two: Right and wrong are defined by my own self-interest; right is what makes me happy, wrong is what doesn't.
- Stage three: Right and wrong are socially determined, and in order to fit into my peer group I follow its norms.
- Stage four: Right and wrong are liberated from society and rest in immutable laws that must be followed.
- Stage five: Right and wrong are measured by a sense of individual rights. Although moral laws still exist, there are situations in which they must be broken in order to act according to a higher principle.
- Stage six: Right and wrong are determined by my own set of self-chosen principles and guidelines that are elevated above those laws set by society.

Although Kohlberg admitted few people ever reach stage six, he was willing to posit a theoretical stage seven, transcendental morality, linking morality with religion.[1]

Kohlberg's theory has been challenged by a number of scholars and researchers over the years, most notably by Carol Gilligan. Noting that Kohlberg's study focuses exclusively on boys, Gilligan offers a different sense of moral development that includes girls. Where Kohlberg argues that the highest stage of moral development is one that lifts you out of the situation to follow your own independently reasoned notion of right and wrong, Gilligan notes that girls do not value the lone-ranger ideal and place relationships at the heart of moral reasoning.[2] In other words, Kohlberg's boys lean naturally toward zero-sum thinking, while Gilligan's girls lean naturally toward nonzero thinking.

My goal here is not to argue for or against Kohlberg or Gilligan, but simply to note that both assume that moral choice is an act of free will and that the individual actor has the potential to reach the highest level of moral decision making, whether this be Kohlberg's stage six (or seven) or Gilligan's relational awareness. Is this assumption valid? Can we remove the individual actor from the scene in which the action takes place and allow her or him to apply abstract ideals—philosophical or relational—to the situation? Or are the actor and the play inseparable?

If the former is true, then one can argue that anyone can apply the Golden Rule in any situation simply by an act of will: freeing yourself from the predilections of nature, nurture, and society and doing to others regardless of what others are doing to you. If the latter is true, if the actor and the play are one, then the only way to proceed ethically is to know the self as part of the play rather than to abstract yourself from it.

Again the notion that we have free will, that we are independent agents, assumes, contra *Hamlet*, that the play is not the thing. Science seems to suggest otherwise. Take the 1971 Stanford Prison Experiment, for example. Under the guidance of psychologist Philip Zimbardo, twenty-four male Stanford students were divided into two groups, prisoners and guards, and set in a mock prison situation to see how each group would act. Within forty-eight hours the prisoners began to rebel, while the guards resorted to harsher and harsher treatment of them. Despite the fact that all students were volunteers and that anyone could quit the experiment at any time, only two students quit early on. Given the rising tensions and abuse, the entire experiment was shut down by Zimbardo after only six days.[3]

These were not exceptional students prone to rebellion or abusive behavior. Yet they acquiesced to their roles and the social pressure placed upon them via those roles. Where was the moral free agent? Why didn't anyone think to apply the Golden Rule?

My argument is simple: no one thought to apply the Golden Rule because the Rule was irrelevant to the game. This was a zero-sum game of us against them, and winning and losing was at the heart of the play. The students simply forgot the larger context of their lives. The "guards" became guards and the "prisoners" became prisoners, and both groups forgot they were students volunteering in a psychology experiment. Had they been able to shift perspectives from zero-sum to nonzero, had they been able to move from a finite game of domination and submission to an infinite game of relationship building, the experiment would have gone very differently.

Scholar and author Heidi Ravven, drawing on the Stanford Prisoner Experiment as well as research into the Holocaust and the abuses at Abu Ghraib prison in Iraq, comes to the following conclusion: "The evidence seems to suggest that it is the uncritical adoption of a particular interpretive frame for a given situation that is at the center of perpetration [of evil] when it comes to normal people."[4] In other words, the larger the frame, the larger the chances for acting from the Golden Rule.

In the Stanford Prison Experiment, the Holocaust, and Abu Ghraib, the "other" was demonized and seen as a threat to the self. Abusing or even murdering the other was justified by the frame in which morality was defined.[5] While I may understand that cancer cells are no less a part of me than healthy cells, I still feel no remorse in killing the former to protect the latter. If you can convince me that Jews are a cancer in the Aryan body, as the Nazis convinced people in the 1930s and 1940s, then killing Jews is simply the right thing to do. In short, "social and situational forces rather than free will decision making and stable personal character largely determine what people do, what actions people take, whether they harm or help."[6]

If this is so, then why do we persist in attributing moral agency to the lone individual, what psychologists call the fundamental attribution error? The answer, according to Ravven, is Judeo-Christian-Muslim bias toward free agency:

> Free will is the belief that each of us (unless we are children beneath the "age of reason" or mentally incompetent) has enough independence from history, context, culture, group, present situation, and even biology to enable us, uniquely as a species, to be the originators (in some sense and to some meaningful degree) of our actions, choosing them freely and hence being individually responsible for them. That claim is the standard reason given for why we deserve praise for good actions and blame for bad ones.[7]

The reason free will is so important to us is that without it, the system of reward and punishment in this life, and perhaps more importantly in the next life, makes no sense. This is true whether we are talking about Judaism, Christianity, or Islam, with their similar notions of heaven and hell, or about Hinduism and Buddhism, with their multiple heavens and hells and the idea of reincarnation. In all of these systems individuals are held accountable for their actions and rewarded or punished because of them. If these actions are not freely chosen, then a system of reward and punishment, however defined, would be not only arbitrary but also unjust and mean-spirited.

It is essential to these religious traditions that the individual is a free moral agent, for without this their respective theories of reward and punishment make no sense. As Saint Augustine wrote in *On Genesis*, "The providence of God rules and administers the whole creation, both natures and wills: natures in order to give them existence, wills so that those that are good may not be without merit, and those that are evil may not go unpunished."[8] To be a free moral agent you must be free from any inherent bias toward good or evil rooted in nature or the human body. Again Saint Augustine: "No one suffers punishment for faults of nature, but for vices of the will; for even the vice which has come to seem natural because strengthened by habit or because it has taken an undue hold derives its origin from the will."[9]

The point Saint Augustine is making, and the point all believers in free will have to make in one way or another, is that you can rise above the limitations of history, biology, and social setting and act by pure will for good or for ill. In fact, all moral action can only be willed action, even if your will is simply to acquiesce to peer pressure. The isolated free agent with limitless free will within the moral sphere is essential to this kind of thinking, but it cannot be proved and is most likely a fiction created by a theological zero-sum game of winners and losers, saved and damned.

Lest you think this notion of free will is unique to Augustine and Christianity, listen to the medieval Jewish philosopher Maimonides on the subject:

The Holy One, Blessed Be He, knows everything that will happen before it has happened. So does He know whether a particular person will be righteous or wicked, or not? If He does know, then it will be impossible for that person not to be righteous. If He knows that he will be righteous but that it is possible for him to be wicked, then He does not know everything that He has created....

The Holy One, Blessed Be He, does not have any temperaments and is outside such realms, unlike people, whose selves and temperaments are two separate things. God and His temperaments are one, and God's existence is beyond the comprehension of Man....

[Thus] we do not have the capabilities to comprehend how the Holy One, Blessed Be He, knows all creations and events. [Nevertheless] we know without doubt that people do what they want without the Holy One, Blessed Be He, forcing or decreeing upon them to do so.... It has been said because of this that a man is judged according to all his actions.[10]

Yes, it is said, but is it true? Can you free yourself from the conditioning of biology, psychology, and sociology to act freely from a blank slate? I don't think so.

When it comes to questions of moral agency I am, if you will, a Taoist. I believe that you and I are part of a larger, perhaps infinite system of rising and falling, birthing and dying, and I believe that good and bad, right and wrong are elements of this system and no more separate from one another than front is separate from back or up is separate from down. Our sense of self is limited only by our capacity to see nature as it is: interdependent parts composing a dynamic whole. You and I are part of and never apart from this whole. Hence we cannot extricate ourselves from the larger context in which we function in order to make moral judgments outside the influence of the larger context.

For me, the key to making good moral choices isn't to extricate myself from the system in which I "live and move and have my being," to borrow from Saint Paul in Acts 17:28, but to understand that system more and more accurately. It is wisdom rather than will that forms the basis of good moral decision making.

Wisdom refers to our capacity to understand the reality of which we are a part and in which we find ourselves. Will is the capacity to shape that reality to our desires. While we may have some rudimentary capacity for shaping reality, this capacity doesn't extend to moral choices. As we have seen in a variety of cases, it is the situation that shapes us rather than we who shape the situation. If this is so, and I think it is, then when it comes to making moral choices we are better served by understanding the larger reality of which we are a part than we are by seeking to impose our desire or will on that reality.

What is this larger reality? It is the infinite nonzero system of birthing and dying in which and of which everything happens. When we understand reality, our moral choices naturally shift from finite zero-sum to infinite nonzero, and the Golden Rule becomes the optimal guide for living.

Heidi Ravven, whose book *The Self beyond Itself* informs much of my own thinking in this matter, calls this pitting the true against the good. Rather than imagining an abstract and universal idea of the good—something akin to Immanuel Kant's categorical imperative, a moral stance that should be incumbent upon all people at all times—I suggest you investigate to see what is true about the situation in which you find yourself. What you will find is this: you are playing either a finite zero-sum game, or you are playing an infinite nonzero game. If the former, then what is good is what ends the game at the other's expense. If the latter, then what is good is what maintains the game for the benefit of both you and the other.

If you are playing a finite game, then the Golden Rule is irrelevant, something we have seen over and over, but—and this is a very important "but"—its very irrelevance is a red flag calling you to notice the finite game and the zero-sum nature of your situation. Once you are aware of the truth, you can look even further to see whether this finite zero-sum game is in your long-term best interest. In other words, is playing a finite game harming your standing in the larger infinite game of life? If it is—in my own life I find this to be the case almost every time—then you have the opportunity to operate not from the narrow mind-set of finite zero-sum mentality, but from the spacious mind-set of infinite nonzero mentality instead. The shift is made not by an act of will but as a consequence of wisdom.

Notice I didn't say that when you see the harm a finite game may be doing to your long-term well-being, you choose to shift from finite zero-sum to infinite nonzero. That would be an act of will, something I doubt we have in sufficient quantity to make this shift. I am saying that knowing the truth in and of itself makes the shift happen. As Jesus said, "And you will know the truth, and the truth will make you free" (John 8:32). The *truth* will set you free, not the will. This is the view of the Jewish philosopher Baruch Spinoza (1632–1677).

> It was Spinoza's brainstorm that the moral path was not from selfish isolated individualism to altruism via a free will, but instead from a diffuse localism in which self and environment were merged to an expansive identification with worlds and environments further and further afield yet understood as having combined to produce this unique "me."[11]

This shift is not an act of will but an expansion of wisdom. What Spinoza is calling for is for you to look deeply into your reality and see that the self you imagine yourself to be is a tiny fragment of the true self you really are. The imagined self is isolated, finite, and prone to zero-sum thinking. The true self is organic, infinite, and naturally given to nonzero thinking. The shift from one self to the other requires not an act of will but a maturation of wisdom. As our wisdom grows, so too does our predisposition to the Golden Rule.

> It was this transformation toward an enlarged and coherent self—a self extended by its constitution and by its relations with the world, distributed into its environments, and systematically integrated—that Spinoza envisioned as capable of true moral agency.[12]

Wisdom rather than will is the key to moral agency, to living a moral life defined as one that acts in ways that are beneficial to the infinite whole of which we are each a part.

When I teach this to kids I often do the following: I pass out small bags of candy-coated chocolates, asking only that the children keep the bag sealed and held in their right hands. Once the candy is distributed, I ask the children how it is that they are keeping their left hand from attacking the right hand to wrest the candy from it. Naturally they think I am crazy. As I recall one eight-year-old girl saying to me, "That makes no sense. My left hand doesn't want to attack my right hand because my left hand knows that the candy belongs to all of me."

Exactly. No act of will is needed to keep one hand from attacking the other because we are wise enough to know that both hands are "me." The left hand naturally does to the right hand what the left hand would want the right hand to do to it because someone knows that left and right are part of a greater unity; working in harmony with one another is in the best interest of both.

What Spinoza is saying, and what I am arguing in this book, is that the wiser you are, the more you see your "self" as the other, indeed as all others. And as you do, your actions regarding these others will naturally follow the principle of the Golden Rule.

As I unpack the candy-coated chocolates example to the class, someone almost always asks, "Why then have a Golden Rule at all?" Why indeed? If I can't will myself into compliance with the Rule, then why have the Rule in the first place? My answer is that the purpose of the Golden Rule is not to demand obedience but to encourage wise inquiry. We use the Rule as a way of testing the quality of our wisdom.

When I look to see whether my actions are in accordance with the Golden Rule, what it reveals to me is the degree to which I am wise enough to see the infinite nonzero reality in which I operate. The Rule is a gauge allowing me to read where I am on the scale from finite to infinite games and zero-sum to nonzero thinking. The more natural the Rule seems, the more I am living on the infinite nonzero side of the spectrum. The more unnatural the Rule seems, the more I am living on the finite zero-sum side of the spectrum. The Rule tells me where I am, not what to do. What to do is always the same: enhance my wisdom to better know the truth. If I do that, the Rule will take care of itself.

9

Living the Rule

Toward a Global Ethic

Let's begin with a brief summary of what we have learned thus far in this exploration of the Golden Rule. The notion of doing or not doing to others as you would or would not have them do to you rests on your understanding of just who this "you" is. As we have seen, there are two basic ways to answer the question "Who am I?" One way sets in motion the infinite nonzero Game of Black-*and*-White; the other sets in motion the finite zero-sum Game of Black-*or*-White. The first way sees all life as a single system of relationships among and between interdependent parts where the success of each is dependent on the success of all; the second way sees life as a competition between often mutually antagonistic factions. The first will value the Golden Rule as essential to the maintenance of the infinite game in which it finds itself; the second will find the Golden Rule a silly distraction from winning the finite game it is playing.

When you try to calculate what is ethical, good, and just, you are actually determining which kind of self you see yourself to be and which game you are playing. To the extent you see yourself as a separate self in competition with all other selves, you will find the Golden Rule irrelevant. As we have been arguing throughout this book, the Golden Rule only makes sense when you see yourself as part of a single system of life, a universal, perhaps even cosmic, infinite nonzero game.

You Are an Infinite Nonzero Game

Chances are when asked to point to your body you would turn your finger toward your chest or your head. Very few of us would point to a nearby tree or to the sun or to the earth beneath our feet. Yet these are no less essential parts of our body as any organ within our head or chest.

Consider your lungs, for example. Clearly they are an essential part of you. Without them you would die. Yet lungs alone are insufficient to carry your self or sense of "you." Your lungs are a mechanism for exchanging gases. They remove carbon dioxide from your body and take oxygen into your body, but your lungs do not produce either gas. Let's focus on oxygen.

Without oxygen you will die. Getting oxygen into your bloodstream is the work of your lungs. But making the oxygen you so desperately need has nothing to do with your lungs or you at all. At least not the "you" you take yourself to be when you answer the question "Who are you?" by pointing to your chest.

Oxygen is produced through photosynthesis, the process plants, algae, and trees use to transform the energy of sunlight into chemical energy necessary for life. One of the essential by-products of photosynthesis—essential to us humans, at any rate—is oxygen. Oxygen hardly existed on earth prior to the evolution of plants capable of photosynthesis some 3.5 billion years ago, and sufficient amounts of oxygen to support aerobic life didn't arrive until 2.4 billion years ago. This is called the Great Oxygenation Event and was a boon for aerobic organisms but caused the extinction of many anaerobic ones.

So your lungs need oxygen to function. Since that is so, why limit your understanding of lungs to the lungs alone? Why not speak of the lung-oxygen system? And since oxygen is a by-product of photosynthesis and photosynthesis needs plants, trees, and algae to interact with the light from the sun, your lungs are also dependent on these. Trees, plants, algae, and sunlight are no less a vital organ of "you" than your lungs. Trees, plants, and algae need water and earth to survive, so we will have to add these to "you" as well. A quick survey of the geography of earth's neighboring planets suggests that the amount of water and sunlight we need must fall within a certain range, a range provided by planet earth's relation to the sun. The earth is where it is because the other planets are where they are—gravity holding us in the life-producing sweet spot. So the solar system is also "you."

We could continue our expansion of your body until we would have to say that the entire universe is you, but I will leave that exploration up to you. Suffice it to say that your body is far more than what is contained in the bag of skin you might point to when pointing to "you."

If this is true of the physical "you," then can it also be true of the emotional and psychological "you" as well? Are thoughts and feelings something you produce, or are they something to which you relate as they arise in you? You are capable of processing emotion and thought just as you are capable of processing carbon dioxide and oxygen, but you don't produce thoughts and feelings any more than you produce oxygen or carbon dioxide.

The notion that we don't produce—and hence control—our own thoughts and feelings may be more difficult to accept than the fact that we don't produce oxygen. So check it out for yourself. Do you, the conscious and self-conscious "you" you take yourself to be, construct thoughts and feelings, or do you react to them as they arise fully constructed into your field of awareness?

Think of the last time you were moved to tears. This happens to me quite often. YouTube clips of adorable puppies can send tears rolling down my cheeks, but I'm only aware of how the puppy videos affect my feelings after the effect has happened. I don't choose to be moved or to tear up; I just do.

The same is true of thoughts. As you read the words on this page, you are having emotional and intellectual reactions. You will, most likely, claim these as your own and assume that you react the way you do because you choose to react the way you do. But is this really the case? Are you thinking about the ideas being presented because you want to or because they are arising of their own accord as a by-product of reading?

Of course, if you don't like what you are experiencing as you read this book, you can choose to put the book aside and stop reading, and when you do, the feelings and thoughts will change, but that only proves my point. The only way to avoid reacting to the input of this book is to avoid having a relationship with the book. Just as your body is a system of interdependent relationships with the world of matter, gas, and energy, so your mind—emotional and intellectual—is a system of interdependent relationships with the worlds of thought and feeling.

Tanking the "I"

We may imagine that thoughts and feelings arise in our minds and are in this way independent of the world outside our minds, but is this really the case? If you lacked any input from the outside, would you continue to generate thoughts and feelings from the inside?

I spent many months exploring this question through the use of sensory deprivation tanks. Despite the popularity of the 1980 sci-fi horror movie *Altered States*, the use of such tanks doesn't cause devolution of human consciousness and the emergence of a Mr. Hyde–like character. On the contrary, the promise of sensory deprivation was to trigger an evolution of consciousness beyond the ego to the greater "I" that embraces all life. My own experience was somewhere in between.

The tanks I used were essentially sound- and light-proof coffins filled with a few inches of water heated to body temperature and containing a high concentration of Epsom salts. Lying naked in the tank was like floating on a waterbed without the plastic sheet. Once the lid of the tank is closed, I was immersed in ... well, nothingness. Unless I stretched out my arms to touch the sides of the tank itself, within minutes I was floating weightless in infinite nothingness. No light, no sound, no touch, no taste—nothing to stimulate my mind from outside the brain.

In the months I spent periodically immersing myself in these tanks I was seeking enlightenment. My hope was that I could achieve the state of no-mind that my Zen teachers seemed to value without having to spend years sitting cross-legged on kapok-stuffed cushions. This isn't what happened.

Although I did my best to maintain some sense of awareness during my hour-long sensory deprivation sessions, the fact is I couldn't do so at all. As I settled into the emptiness around me, I fell into a state of egoless hallucinations. I saw abstract shapes in colors I didn't see in the outside world. There were snippets of dreams and echoes of what, for a moment, seemed like profound revelations, but all this passed quickly and "I" disappeared. Without any relationship with the outside, there was no sense of "I" on the inside.

What I took from these hours of investigation was this: there is no independent "I" separate from the world. What sense of "I" there is results from my physical engagement with the world. Not exactly "I am the world," but more that "the world is me." To paraphrase Zen teacher Alan Watts, we are not separate and independent beings *in* the world; we are specific (and temporary) actions *of* the world.[1] Without that world we don't exist.

> It is essential to understand this point thoroughly: that the thing-in-itself (Kant's *ding an sich*), whether animal, vegetable, or mineral, is not only unknowable—it does not exist.... Individual people, nations, animals, insects, and plants do not exist in or by themselves. This is not to say only that things exist in relation to one another, but that what we call "things" are no more than glimpses of a unified process.[2]

This realization is central to a deeper understanding of the Golden Rule and its predecessors such as the command "Love your neighbor as yourself" (Leviticus 19:18). If we imagine this "self" to be a thing unto itself, independent of other selves, and condemned to live in a world of competing selves, then using this self as a benchmark of morality is highly problematic. First, can it even be done? Can I love someone else as much as I love myself? Can I really do to them what I would like them to do to me? Or am I more inclined to do to them just enough to get them to do to me what I want done?

Of course there are examples of altruism where a mother, for example, will sacrifice herself for her child, but these stand out because they are so rare. Even when they do occur, people like Selfish Gene will argue that this isn't a conscious act of self-sacrifice but a genetic imperative, with mom "knowing" that the perpetuation of her genetic line rests with the survival of her offspring, and so she will do whatever it takes—even die—to see to that survival.

Even if I can do to others what I want them to do to me, the task itself is self-contradictory. What I want is to win, even if winning means nothing more than survival. In a zero-sum world of competing selves, my winning depends on and necessitates others' losing. That is the nature of finite zero-sum games. So if I do to others what I want them to do to me, I find myself promoting their winning, which can only be done at the expense of my own winning, which is contrary to what I want.

In short: you cannot love another as yourself when ultimate self-love requires that you triumph over other selves in the finite zero-sum game of life.

If, on the other hand, we realize that there are not individual selves, that we are each unique expressions of a singular process, an infinite game of happening, of life birthing and dying, succeeding and failing, rising and falling, and the rest, then the self that defines us all *is* us all. Loving my neighbor as myself is the realization that my neighbor is myself and I am my neighbor and we both are the happening that embraces and transcends all things.

Tat Tvam Asi: **Thou Art That**

"Doing to others" in this context means acting in a way that maintains the game. Remember, in infinite games there are no winners and losers. The goal of the game is to keep the game going. As long as the game survives, we all win. If the game ends, we all lose.

Imagine the game here is the happening we call life, existence, reality. What I want done to me is whatever keeps me going as optimally as possible. What I will do to you is whatever keeps you going as optimally as possible. As long as we act in this way the game keeps going and we all win. The play's the thing, as Shakespeare reminded us in *Hamlet*.

The key to playing the infinite game is understanding that you and I and all other happenings of the Great Happening that is life are one. As the eighth-century-BCE Chandogya Upanishad puts it: *Tat tvam asi*, "You are that" (Chandogya Upanishad 6.8.7). And yet you are also this.

Don't imagine that the body that seems to be you is other than the body you truly are. The body you appear to be is simply part of the greater body that is all bodies.

We can understand this in the context of figure/ground (see Diagram 1). No doubt you have seen these kinds of diagrams before, where two images are present and yet only one can be grasped at a time. One of the most common is the goblet/face image:

[Diagram 1]

When we focus on the figure of the white goblet, the two faces disappear into the ground. When we focus on the black faces, the goblet disappears into the ground. It isn't that the goblet is superior to the faces or that the faces are superior to the goblet, it is that we cannot see both at the same time. Pitting one against the other, privileging one over the other, is the Game of Black-*or*-White (figure *or* ground). It is a game played in ignorance—indeed it can only be played by ignoring one in favor of the other and refusing to realize that one and the other go together and cannot in fact be separated.

Seeking to separate them, trying to have the goblet win and the faces lose, or the faces win and the goblet lose, can only result in the end of both. Realizing that the diagram itself is figure *and* ground rather than figure *versus* ground allows us to realize that while it may be impossible for us to see both at once, it is foolish for us to pit one against the other. Rather, we must see that for either to win (survive), both must win. This is the Game of Black-*and*-White. It is an infinite nonzero game that sees to the welfare of each by seeing to the welfare of both.

When we apply the Golden Rule, we do so in the context of an infinite game. Altruism isn't necessary because selfishness no longer leads to the dualism of I against Thou, or Us against Them. There is only I/ Thou and Us/Them. Or, to put it most boldly: there is only the nondual I that embraces and transcends the seemingly dual us. Being for myself in this context means being for everyone and everything, for that is what we now understand "self" to be.

You Are a Verb

One of the reasons it is so difficult for us to understand the true nature of self is the language we use regarding it. "Self" is a noun, but if we look closely at the world and ourselves, we will find no nouns at all, only verbs. There are no doers in the world; there are only doings. There are no nouns, only verbs. Action is not something added to an inactive thing; action is what it is to be anything at all.

When you look at a tree, for example, do you see a static thing or a living process, a "tree" or "tree-ing"? When you see a dog, do you see a static being or a living process, a "dog-ing"? I suggest that the latter is the case every time. There is nothing doing anything; there is only doing that is everything.

The confusion arises from our language. We say, "It is raining" as if there were an object, an "it" separate from the act of raining. There isn't. There is only raining. It would help intellectually and spiritually, though it would be very awkward grammatically, to speak without nouns. Gerunds would be the norm, replacing names and nouns of all kinds. I would no longer be Rami but Rami-ing. I wouldn't have a self; I would be self-ing.

Now take this back to the command to love our neighboring as our selfing. Do you see it? There is only selfing, here as neighbor there as you. To care for the one is to care for them both, for they are inseparable.

> The world cannot be analyzed correctly into distinct parts; instead, it must be regarded as an indivisible unit in which separate parts appear as valid approximations only in the classical [i.e., Newtonian] limit.... Thus, at the quantum level of accuracy, an object does not have any "intrinsic" properties (for instance, wave or particle) belonging to itself alone; instead, it shares all its properties mutually and indivisibly with the systems with which it interacts.[3]

The point the eminent physicist David Bohm is making here isn't that there are no happenings; there clearly are. His point is that there is no "thing" happening, just the happening itself. The infinite game of life is a nonzero game, and to play it well is to play in a way that keeps the happening happening. And for that Professor Joshua Greene, director of Harvard's Moral Cognition Lab, tells us there is no better guide than the Golden Rule:

> We can argue about rights and justice forever, but we are bound together by two more basic things. First, we are bound together by the ups and downs of the human experience. We all want to be happy. None of us wants to suffer. Second, we all understand the Golden Rule and the ideal of impartiality behind it. Put these two ideas together and we have a common currency, a system for making principled compromises.[4]

Greene's reference to "impartiality" is what we are calling nonzero. You cannot elevate self over other when abiding by the Golden Rule. Indeed, doing so always shifts us from infinite nonzero games to finite zero-sum games.

A Global Ethic

Catholic theologian Hans Küng presented a "Declaration toward a Global Ethic" at the Parliament of the World's Religions held in Chicago, Illinois, in 1993. His hope was to engage the sixty-five hundred participants at the parliament in an effort to articulate a set of ethical standards shared by all the world's religions and spark a conversation within, between, and among religions as humanity seeks to fashion an ethic for the global village. At the heart of this declaration is the Golden Rule:

> There is a principle which is found and has persisted in many religious and ethical traditions of humankind for thousands of years: *What you do not wish done to yourself, do not do to others.* Or in positive terms: *What you wish done to yourself, do to others!* This should be the irrevocable, unconditional norm for all areas of life, for families and communities, for races, nations, and religions.[5]

Küng offers no other rationale for his claim that the Golden Rule "should be the irrevocable, unconditional norm for all areas of life." He simply takes this as axiomatic, bolstered perhaps by the fact that the Rule is so ubiquitous. Yet, as we have seen, there is nothing unquestionable about the Rule at all. In fact, the Golden Rule, at least in our estimation, is counterintuitive, a fact that becomes all the more obvious in the paragraph following the affirmation of the Golden Rule as the bedrock of a global ethic:

> Every form of egoism should be rejected: all selfishness, whether individual or collective, whether in the form of class thinking, racism, nationalism, or sexism. We condemn these because they prevent humans from being authentically human.[6]

The global ethic is clearly utopian, which, I suspect, is why some twenty years after the proposal of a global ethic the world has yet to accept one. The reason for this, as we have argued throughout this book, is simple: the Golden Rule is golden only in the context of infinite nonzero games, and the world prefers to play finite zero-sum games instead. This doesn't negate the value of the Rule, but it does make the case that if you want to live by the Rule you will have to shift from finite zero-sum games to infinite nonzero ones.

While not explicitly articulating this understanding of the Golden Rule, Küng in fact takes it as his starting point. Just after asserting "there is an irrevocable, unconditional norm for all areas of life, for families and communities, for races, nations, and religions,"[7] and just before revealing that this norm is the Golden Rule, the "Declaration toward a Global Ethic" states:

> We are interdependent. Each of us depends on the well-being of the whole, and so we have respect for the community of living beings, for people, animals, and plants, and for the preservation of Earth, the air, water, and soil.[8]

The affirmation of the interdependence of all life is the affirmation of life as an infinite game. Accepting that the well-being of each depends on the well-being of all is an affirmation of nonzero thinking. Only when these two positions are accepted as true can we then move on to the Golden Rule as foundational to a global ethic. Because making this shift is so difficult, Küng's global ethic is still a work in progress.

Widening the Circle

I confess that I find the interdependence of life beyond dispute. Because this is so, I find the Golden Rule essential and Küng's global ethic intrinsically compelling. Indeed, we might say that accepting the first makes accepting the second and third inevitable. Sadly, this doesn't work in reverse. If it did, if the Golden Rule led to infinite nonzero thinking and interaction, then we would not see the world's religions condoning and often promoting its opposite. Yet they do.

This fact doesn't mean the Golden Rule is wrong, only that it is infinite nonzero thinking and not the Rule itself that is foundational. Once the former is accepted, the latter becomes the norm. Without that acceptance, the Golden Rule is just another ideal observed more in the breaking than in the keeping.

Because this is so, the first step in living the Golden Rule is changing the games we play. Hans Küng seems to recognize this when he speaks of all humanity as being one family:

> We consider humankind our family. We must strive to be kind and generous. We must not live for ourselves alone, but should also serve others, never forgetting the children, the aged, the poor, the suffering, the disabled, the refugees, and the lonely. No person should ever be considered or treated as a second-class citizen, or be exploited in any way whatsoever. There should be equal partnership between men and women. We must not commit any kind of sexual immorality. We must put behind us all forms of domination or abuse.[9]

Considering all humankind to be our family is not the norm in the world's religions or in other human groupings. Religions and nation-states often obsess over in-group and out-group. As we saw in our discussion of the idea of "neighbor" and "stranger" in Leviticus, at no point did any commentator up to and including early modernity suggest that these words referred to all humanity. To the Jewish authors and commentators, your neighbor was your fellow Jew-by-birth and the "stranger" was your fellow Jew-by-conversion. Non-Jews, even if they lived next door, were not included in either category.

Similarly in Islam, the world is divided into two spheres: *Dar al-Harb* and *Dar al-Islam*, the World of War and the World of Peace, or the non-Muslim and Muslim worlds, respectively. In Christianity we have the saved and the damned; in Hinduism, the divisions of caste and subcaste. Although I agree that considering all humanity as one family is essential to both the Golden Rule and any global ethic, I think it wise to make clear that this notion is radical and far from settled. Further, if a truly global ethic is to emerge, then I suggest we expand the circle of family even wider to include all life, for as we have seen, humanity is not independent of the biosphere in which we arise and live.

In 1877 the Irish historian William Lecky wrote:

> The moral unity to be expected in different ages is not a unity of standard or of acts, but a unity of tendency.... At one time the benevolent affections embrace merely the family, soon the circle expanding includes first a class, then a nation, then a coalition of nations, then all humanity, and finally, its influence is felt in the dealings of man with the animal world.[10]

We have yet to achieve this level of identification. But the question isn't just "Have we reached it?" but "Is it possible for us to reach it?" Can we humans see ourselves as part of the whole and therefore act ethically toward it? As bioethicist Peter Singer explains in *The Expanding Circle: Ethics, Evolution, and Moral Progress*:

> An ethic for human beings must take them as they are, or as they have some chance of becoming. If the manner of our evolution has made our feelings for our kin, and for

those who have helped us, stronger than our feelings for our fellow humans in general, an ethic that asks each of us to work for the good of all will be cutting against the grain of human nature. The goal of maximizing the welfare of all may be better achieved by an ethic that accepts our inclinations and harnesses them so that, taken as a whole, the system works for everyone's advantage.[11]

A system that works for everyone is an infinite nonzero game. So now the question is "Can people play such a game?" No, let me amend that. The question is "Can *you* play such a game?"

Can you see that you are part of a larger circle? How large is that circle? Let's assume it includes your immediate family, but how far beyond that does it extend? Can you see your interdependence with the people of your town, state, and country? Can you widen it out beyond nationality? What about race, gender, ethnicity? Is that your limit? Or can you embrace all humankind as kin? And then there is the animal world, and the bioregion in which you live. And then earth and the cosmos beyond. How far can you expand your circle of interdependence and hence your circle of concern as well?

The widening of your circle is an ongoing process. The more you know about the reality in which you function, the wider your circle will grow. That is why so many of us choose not to know anything beyond a certain point. That is why many of us hunker down in one silo or another, be it the silo of nationality, race, religion, or ethnicity.

Who is the "them" when you speak of "us and them"? Ultimately there is no "them" and only "us." At that point all games are infinite and all ethics is nonzero. At that point the Golden Rule is the only rule. But that point hasn't yet arrived. So ask yourself: Can it? Will it? And how can you will it in your own life?

From Other to Neighbor; from Neighbor to Self

We began our look at the Golden Rule with a brief reference to Leviticus 19:18, "Love your neighbor as yourself." My aim at that point was to merely make the observation that regardless of the love we profess, our life will be ruled by other emotions. If our neighbor is similar to us, then loving them isn't all that difficult. If our neighbor is different—in race, creed, color, ethnicity, sexual orientation, religion, nationality—then loving them is often very difficult. This is implicit in the relation of "neighbor" to "self" in the obligation to love our neighbor as ourself.

Leviticus 19:18 doesn't command you to love your neighbor as you love yourself; that is closer to the standard Golden Rule. Leviticus commands you to love your neighbor as yourself: to see your neighbor as part of yourself. This is, as I have striven to show, classic nonzero thinking. As we mature into nonzero thinking and infinite play, the other is an extension of self, and the self is an extension of other. This, as Alan Watts made clear, is the infinite Game of Black-and-White.

The ultimate widening of the circle of concern is to see the other—near and far, human and otherwise—as neighbor.

To make my case as clear as I can, let's take a look at one of the greatest critics of "Love your neighbor," Sigmund Freud:

> Let us adopt a naïve attitude towards ["Love your neighbor as your self"], as though we were hearing it for the first time; we shall be unable then to suppress a feeling of surprise and bewilderment. Why should we do it? What good will it do us? But, above all, how shall we achieve it? How can it be possible? My love is something valuable to me which I ought not to throw away without reflection. It imposes duties on me for whose fulfillment I must be ready to make sacrifices. If I love someone, he must deserve it in some way.... But if I am to love him (with this universal love) merely because he, too, is an inhabitant of this earth, like an insect, an earth-worm or a grass-snake, then I fear that only a small modicum of my love will fall to his share—not by any possibility as much as by the judgement [sic] of my reason, I am entitled to retain for myself. What is the point of a precept enunciated with so much solemnity if its fulfillment cannot be recommended as reasonable?[12]

Freud's naïve approach to "Love your neighbor" is what we are call-ing zero-sum. He sees the neighbor as alien to himself. To Freud, the one-sided nature of the Rule—that is, loving your neighbor regardless of who your neighbor is or what your neighbor does—leads him to a notion of the neighbor that is highly negative:

> He seems not to have the least trace of love for me and shows me not the slightest consideration. If it will do him any good he has no hesitation injuring me, nor does he ask himself whether the amount of advantage he gains bears any proportion to the extent of the harm he does me. Indeed, he need not even obtain an advantage, if he can satisfy any sort of desire by it, he thinks nothing of jeering at me, insulting me, slandering me and showing his superior power; and the more secure he feels and the more helpless I am, the more certainly I can expect him to behave like this to me.[13]

Freud goes on to assume that his neighbor, when asked to love Sigmund as himself, will respond with the same sense of outrage. The only reason you should love another is if the other loves you. Since one's love of the other is dependent on the other's love for you, and vice versa, there is no hope that either will ever love the other at all. Someone has to love first and for no reason, and that, at least according to Freud, just isn't going to happen.

Given that Freud is a Jew living in a hostile environment steeped in anti-Semitism, we might be inclined to cut him a bit of slack, but doing so would undermine the very Rule we seek to applaud. It is precisely in a hostile environment that the Golden Rule is to be lived, because doing so is the means by which we might help shift relationships from zero-sum to nonzero. Freud of course rejects this out of hand:

> Civilization pays no attention to all this; it merely admon-ishes us that the harder it is to obey the precept the more meritorious it is to do so. But anyone who follows such a precept in present-day civilization only puts himself at a disadvantage vis-à-vis the person who disregards it.[14]

As far as Freud is concerned, the only advantage one might have for living by the precept "Love your neighbor" is the "narcissistic satisfaction of being able to think oneself better than others."[15] This is why, he continues, religions shift moral argument from this world to the next. The only reward religions can offer those willing to take "Love your neighbor" as their moral standard is one restricted to the afterlife. Why? Because in this world living by this precept only sets you up to be victimized by the very neighbor you are trying to love.

Freud is speaking from, and is a wonderful spokesman for, zero-sum thinking and finite game playing. All the more so when you know he, as a Jew, is on the losing end of that finite game. His morality is decidedly zero-sum when he quotes German poet and essayist Heinrich Heine as his guide:

> Mine is a most peaceable disposition. My wishes are: a humble cottage with a thatched roof, but a good bed, good food, the freshest milk and butter, flowers before my window, and a few fine trees before my door; and if God wants to make my happiness complete, he will grant me the joy of seeing some six or seven of my enemies hanging from those trees. Before their death I shall, moved in my heart, forgive them all the wrong they did me in their lifetime. One must, it is true, forgive one's enemies—but not before they have been hanged.[16]

From the zero-sum perspective of finite games, Heine and Freud make perfect sense. Asking that one play a finite zero-sum game by the rules of an infinite nonzero game is asking too much. This is why I am arguing for something else.

Whenever possible, shift from the zero-sum to the nonzero, from the finite game to the infinite game. Whenever possible, place the ongoing relationship with your neighbor, human and otherwise, above the temporary game of defeating them.[17] In this way the Golden Rule is not only a moral guide for living in an infinite nonzero world but also a means for shifting out of a finite zero-sum one.

Ubuntu

Coming from the sub-Saharan language group called Bantu, *ubuntu*, "personhood," defines the individual as being part of a collective. Similar to Thich Nhat Hanh's "inter-being," *ubuntu* suggests that you are you only in relation to others. *Ubuntu*, however, isn't only an ontological principle; it is also a character trait similar to *jen*, "humanness," in the Confucian tradition. A person who understands oneself to be a blending of personal rights and communal responsibilities "has *ubuntu*."

> [*Ubuntu*] speaks of the very essence of being human. When we want to give high praise to someone we say, "*Yu u nobuntu*"; "Hey, so-and-so has *ubuntu*." Then you are generous, you are hospitable, you are friendly and caring and compassionate. You share what you have. It is to say, "My humanity is caught up, is inextricably bound up, in yours." We belong in a bundle of life. We say, "A person is a person through other persons." It is not, "I think therefore I am." It says rather: "I am human because I belong. I participate, I share." A person with *ubuntu* is open and available to others, affirming of others, does not feel threatened that others are able and good, for he or she has a proper self-assurance that comes from knowing that he or she belongs to a greater whole and is diminished when others are humiliated or diminished, when others are tortured or oppressed, or treated as if they were less than who they are.[18]

Ubuntu is the quality of living in an infinite nonzero universe in which the Golden Rule is the only moral standard we need. One who has *ubuntu* doesn't have to decide between self and other, but rather knows that self and other are part of a single system of life and, knowing this, cannot help but engage with life in a manner that reflects the win-win attitude of infinite nonzero play. As Michael Battle, author of *Ubuntu: I in You and You in Me*, explains,

> *Ubuntu* recognizes that our need to be seen for who we really are is an existential reality in which we need to be

part of something larger than ourselves. *Ubuntu* also helps
us see that we need to be part of a community with a
measure of mutuality and like-mindedness.[19]

This notion that my "self" is not mine but somehow "ours" poses a
grave threat to finite zero-sum thinking. Without a "them," there is
no "us." Without the saved, there are no damned; without the chosen,
there are no gentiles; without the true believer, there are no heretics;
without the wise, there are no fools. If we are each a part of the other,
then we are all chosen and not chosen, saved and damned. Or, to put
the same idea in a positive way, the *ubuntu* mind-set means that "there
is no longer Jew or Greek, there is no longer slave or free, there is no
longer male and female" (Galatians 3:28, NRSV).

Or listen to the wisdom of the thirteenth-century Sufi poet Rumi:

Not Christian or Jew or
Muslim, not Hindu,
Buddhist, Sufi, or Zen.
Not any religion
or cultural system. I am
not from the east
or the west, not
out of the ocean or up
from the ground, not
natural or ethereal, not
composed of elements at all.
I do not exist,
am not an entity in this
world or the next,
did not descend from
Adam and Eve or any
origin story. My place is
the placeless, a trace
of the traceless.
Neither body or soul.
I belong to the beloved,

have seen the two
worlds as one and
that one
call to and know,
first, last, outer, inner,
only that breath breathing
human being.[20]

In the worldview of *ubuntu* "a person is not basically an independent solitary entity." A person is human to the extent that she or he is part of a larger human community and "caught up in the bundle of life. To be is to participate. The *summum bonem* [the highest good] here is not independence but sharing, interdependence."[21]

Or take the teaching of Rabbi Menachem Mendel of Kotzk (1787–1859):

If I am because I am I,
And you are you because you are you, then
I am merely I, and you are merely you.
But if I am I *because* you are you,
And you are you *because* I am I, then
I am not I and you are not you.[22]

Ubuntu argues for a dynamic nonlocal self—a self that isn't reduced to "me" and that must always embrace "you" as well:

[*Ubuntu*] suggests to us that humanity is not embedded
in my person solely as an individual; my humanity is co-
substantively bestowed upon the other and me. Humanity is a quality we owe to each other. We create each
other and need to sustain this *otherness* creation. And if
we belong to each other, we participate in our creations:
we are because you are, and since you are, definitely I am.
The "I am" is not a rigid subject, but a dynamic self-con-
stitution dependent on this *otherness* creation of relation
and distance.[23]

Because our selves commingle with one another in the larger dynamic of selfhood, compassion, the shared suffering of one with another, is self-evident:

> [*Ubuntu*] draws on the fact that we are one human family. We are brothers and sisters, traveling this earth together. When one man is poorly fed, all are malnourished. When one is abused, we all feel the pain. When a child suffers, the tears wash over us all. By recognizing the humanity of one another, we recognize our unbreakable bond—our unbreakable link to the whole of humanity.[24]

My point in bringing *ubuntu* into these reflections on the Golden Rule is not simply for the sake of inclusivity, allowing me to say that Africa, too, has its affirmation of the Golden Rule. *Ubuntu* isn't the African equivalent of the Golden Rule; it is the universal truth that makes the Rule workable.

Most of us live in a competitive zero-sum world where scarcity is promoted and fear of being the loser motivates almost all social, economic, political, and military decision making. Even our religions—all of our religions—while giving lip service to the Golden Rule, tend to observe it largely in the breech because they too operate in a finite zero-sum reality of their own imagining. *Ubuntu* is the opposite of this "fabricated society of competition"[25] and essential to any hope of moving from finite zero-sum living to infinite nonzero loving.

10

Play Different

Shifting the Game

The argument at the heart of this book is fourfold:

1. Humans are game-playing beings—*homo ludens.*
2. We play two types of games: finite zero-sum games and infinite nonzero games.
3. The Golden Rule is the central ethical principle for successfully playing infinite nonzero games but fails miserably in the context of finite zero-sum games.
4. When the Golden Rule fails to apply, we should take this as a reminder to examine the kind and quality of game we are playing and, if necessary, shift from finite zero-sum games to infinite nonzero games.

Notice the caveat "if necessary." I am prejudiced toward infinite nonzero games, but there is a place for finite zero-sum play as well. I enjoy competition and believe that competition can be a catalyst for creativity in many fields of human endeavor, such as economic, artistic, and scientific. But we must place even these areas of winner-take-all zero-sum competition in the larger context of infinite nonzero play so that our winning is not at the expense of our survival as a species. My concern is that we have taken the value of finite zero-sum play to the extreme and applied it across the board in such a way as to be detrimental if not suicidal to all life on this planet.

I set out to write a book that celebrated the Golden Rule as a universal moral compass but found very quickly that my naiveté was blinding me to the truth. The fact that almost every moral system has some version of the Golden Rule would suggest that it is a universal guide, but the fact that these same moral systems violate the Rule whenever they choose to do so makes clear to me that affirming the Golden Rule tells us nothing about one's commitment to living the Rule.

We can print the Golden Rule on posters, tack them up in every classroom on the planet, and still find our morality unaffected. Why? Because the problem isn't that we don't know the Golden Rule; the problem is the games we play render the Rule irrelevant. As long as we promote zero-sum worldviews and play finite games based on these worldviews, we will, as Ron Paul's South Carolina audience did at the 2012 Republican presidential primary debates, boo the Golden Rule even as we insist it comes from the Highest Authority. Even God cannot trump the quality of our games. Indeed, as we have seen, God is often the catalyst for playing the worst kind of games.

If promoting the Golden Rule can't change our morality, what can? Changing the type of game we choose to play.

> When people see themselves in a zero-sum relationship
> with other people—see their fortunes as inversely corre-
> lated with the fortunes of other people, see the dynamic
> as win-lose—they tend to find a scriptural basis for intol-
> erance or belligerence.... When they see the relationship
> as non-zero-sum—see their fortunes as positively corre-
> lated, see the potential for a win-win outcome—they're
> more likely to find the tolerant and understanding side of
> their scriptures.[1]

This is where the Golden Rule becomes the optimal standard of play. In an infinite nonzero game in which each player's success rests on the success of all other players, doing to others as you would have them do to you and not doing to others what you would not want them to do to you become overwhelmingly compelling. The point is that we have to shift the game before we can promote the Rule. This is why teaching morality alone isn't sufficient. Educating ourselves and our children in the Golden Rule without teaching them about finite and infinite games and zero-sum and nonzero worldviews is a waste of time. Doing so would be like teaching them the rules of chess while insisting they play only checkers.

When Congressman Paul suggested a foreign policy based on the Golden Rule, the audience booed. The absurdity of his suggestion was so palpable that the booing was a spontaneous expression of outrage. It was also a spontaneous admission, albeit unintended, that when it comes to our dealings with other nations, especially those we label "the enemy," we see the world in finite zero-sum terms. In the case of Congressman Paul's audience, either the Muslims win or we win, and if we are going to win, we must do to them whatever it takes to make sure they never do to us at all—the Golden Rule be damned.

I applaud the audience's honesty. The question we must ask is this: can we shift games from finite zero-sum to infinite nonzero and in this way learn to accommodate rather than annihilate the "other," or are we doomed by our games to destroy one another completely? I think we can change, and I think the Cuban Missile Crisis proves it.

Most of the Cold War was played as a finite zero-sum game. The goal was to end the game by defeating the other, who in this case was the Soviet Union. The competition between the United States and the Soviet Union was played as winner-take-all. Yet when faced with the realization that they were playing the wrong game, both sides suddenly found the Golden Rule the wiser path to follow. This brief shift came during the Cuban Missile Crisis of October 1962.

In response to the placing of U.S. missiles aimed at Moscow in Turkey and the failed U.S. invasion of Cuba, the Soviets made a secret pact with Cuban dictator Fidel Castro to install Soviet missiles aimed at the United States in Cuba. This was a simple matter of quid pro quo, or doing to the other what the other has already done to you. The action sparked a U.S. blockade of Cuba and a demand for the dismantling of the missiles in Cuba and returning them to the Soviet Union. What played out in public was a finite zero-sum confrontation that could end in a global nuclear catastrophe. Behind the scenes, however, something else was taking place.

At some point the consequences of the game became so stark and unavoidable that the Soviets and Americans changed the game. While the United States and the Soviet Union each declared themselves the winner, the fact was that both were right. The United States won in that the Soviets dismantled their missiles in Cuba and returned them to the Soviet Union. The Soviets won in that the United States publicly declared that it would never again attempt to invade Cuba and privately agreed to remove its missiles from Turkey and Italy. In other words, each did to the other what they wanted the other to do to them.

It isn't that they chose to follow the Golden Rule. It was that they chose to play a different game, an infinite nonzero game, in which the Golden Rule was and is the only way to play.

> This is the way moral evolution happens—in ancient Israel, in the Rome of early Christianity, in Muhammad's Arabia, in the modern world: a people's culture adapts to salient shifts in game-theoretical dynamics by changing its evaluation of the moral status of the people it is playing the game with.[2]

The challenge we humans face is not living up to the Golden Rule but shifting wherever possible from finite zero-sum games to infinite non-zero ones. The questions we must ask of ourselves, our nations, our religions, and our species are as follows:

1. What kind of game are we playing?
2. Is this game in our long-term best interest?

Not every finite zero-sum game is immoral. We would find sporting competitions inane if competing players lowered their level of play to keep their opponents from suffering a defeat that the superior player would not want to suffer. But what works well in a sporting event doesn't work at all in the larger game of life. Most of the games we play should not be played as finite zero-sum games. Whether we are talking about international politics, business, or personal relations, the wiser game is the infinite game, the wiser worldview is the nonzero worldview, and the wiser strategy is the Golden Rule.

Notes

1. The Games People Play: An Introduction to Game Theory

1. Aristotle, *Politics*, trans. C. D. C. Reeve (New York: Hackett, 1998), 6.
2. Florence Scovel Shinn, *The Game of Life and How to Play It* (Camarillo, CA: DeVorss, 1970), 7.
3. Laszlo Mero, *Moral Calculations: Game Theory, Logic, and Human Frailty* (New York: Springer-Verlag, 1998), 28ff.
4. Ibid, 51.
5. Immanuel Kant, *Foundations of the Metaphysics of Morals*, trans. Mary Gregor (Cambridge: Cambridge University Press, 2012), 42.

2. Warning: The Golden Rule May Be Hazardous to Your Faith

1. Swami Vivekananda, *Is Vedanta the Future Religion?* (Kolkata: Advaita Ashrama, 2013), 4–7.
2. Karen Armstrong, *The Great Transformation: The Beginning of Our Religious Traditions* (New York: Alfred A. Knopf, 2006), 392.
3. Karen Armstrong, *Twelve Steps to a Compassionate Life* (New York: Anchor Books, 2010), 6.
4. Ibid, 8.
5. Huston Smith, *The World's Religions* (New York: HarperOne, 2009), 73.
6. Swami Sivananda, "The Unity That Underlies All Religions," cited in Stephen Prothero, *God Is Not One* (New York: HarperCollins, 2010), 2.
7. Peter Singer, *The Expanding Circle: Ethics, Evolution, and Moral Progress* (Princeton, NJ: Princeton University Press, 2011), 160.

3. Evading the Rule in Hinduism, Buddhism, and Confucianism

1. Cited in Bhagavan Das, *Essential Unity of All Religions* (Madras: Theosophical Publishing House, 1955), 404–405; author's rendering.
2. Richard H. Davis, "A Hindu Golden Rule in Context," in *The Golden Rule: The Ethics of Reciprocity in World Religions*, ed. Jacob Neusner and Bruce Chilton (New York: Continuum, 2008), 148.
3. Ibid.
4. Harry Gensler, *Ethics and the Golden Rule* (New York: Routledge, 2013), 49.
5. Bhikkhu Thanissaro, trans., "Nagara Sutta: The City" (SN 12.65), Access to Insight (Legacy Edition), accessed March 10, 2015, www.accesstoinsight.org/tipitaka/sn/sn12/sn12.065.than.html.

6. Thich Nhat Hanh, *The Heart of the Buddha's Teaching* (New York: Broadway Books, 1999), 222.
7. Gensler, *Ethics and the Golden Rule*, 51.
8. Bhikkhu Thanissaro, trans., Samyutta Nikaya Sutra 55:7, Access to Insight (Legacy Edition), accessed March 10, 2015, www.accesstoinsight.org/lib/authors/bodhi/wheel282.html.
9. John Ireland, *The Udana Inspired Utterances of the Buddha* (Kandy, Sri Lanka: Buddhist Publication Society, 1990), 68.
10. Gil Fronsdal, *The Dhammapada: A New Translation of the Buddhist Classic with Annotations* (Boston: Shambhala, 2005), 35.
11. Bhikkhu Bodhi, *The Numerical Discourses of the Buddha: A New Translation of the Anguttara Nikaya* (Boston: Wisdom Publications, 2012), 8:39.
12. Dana MacLean, "Analysis: How to Reverse Buddhism's Radical Turn in Southeast Asia?," *IRIN*, Bangkok, July 16, 2013, www.irinnews.org/report/98423/analysis-how-to-reverse-buddism-s-radical-turn-in-southeast-asia. Up until 2015, IRIN was a service of the UN Office for the Coordination of Humanitarian Affairs. It is currently an independent new service.
13. Ibid.
14. Brian Daizen Victoria, *Zen at War* (New York: Rowman & Littlefield, 2006), xiv.
15. Ibid., 27–28.
16. MacLean, "Analysis."
17. Daisetz T. Suzuki, *Zen and Japanese Culture* (New York: Bollingen Foundation, 1959), 110.
18. Michael Jerryson, "Buddhist Traditions and Violence," in *The Oxford Handbook of Religion and Violence*, ed. Mark Juergensmeyer (New York: Oxford University Press, 2012), 46.
19. *Doctrine of the Mean*, chapter 13, adapted from Jeffrey Wattles, *The Golden Rule* (New York: Oxford University Press, 1996), 18.
20. Robin Wang, *Images of Women in Chinese Thought and Culture: Writings from the Pre-Qin Period through the Song Dynasty* (Indianapolis: Hackett, 2003), 325.

4. Evading the Rule in Judaism, Christianity, and Islam

1. See Harry Gensler, *Ethics and the Golden Rule* (New York: Routledge, 2013), 38–39.
2. Jacob Neusner and Bruce Chilton, eds., *The Golden Rule: The Ethics of Reciprocity in World Religions* (New York: Continuum, 2008), 63.
3. Søren Kierkegaard, *Fear and Trembling* (London: Penguin Books, 1985), 85.
4. Nachmanides, *The Torah with Ramban's Commentary*, vol. 5 (Brooklyn: Mesorah, 2010), 532–533.
5. Samson Raphael Hirsch, *The Hirsch Chumash*, vol. 3, trans. Daniel Haberman (New York: Feldheim Publishers, 2005), 623.
6. Robert D. Putnam, *American Grace: How Religion Divides and Unites Us* (New York: Simon & Schuster, 2010), 443.
7. Ibid., 492.
8. Gensler, *Ethics and the Golden Rule*, 41.
9. *Directorium Inquisitorum* (1578), book 3, 137, column 1, online in the Cornell University Collection, www.digital.library.cornell.edu; also Agostino Borromeo,

"Concerning Nicolas Eymerich's *Directorium Inquisitiorum* and Its 16th-Century Editions," *Critica Storica* 20, no. 4 (1983): 499–547.

10. Martin Luther, *On the Jews and Their Lies*, trans. Domenico d'Abrruzo (Princeton, NJ: Eulenspiegel Press, 2015), 165–168.
11. Barnard Lewis, *Islam: The Religion and the People* (Indianapolis: Wharton Press, 2009), 8.
12. Adapted from Abdel Haleem, trans., *The Qur'an: A New Translation* (Oxford: Oxford University Press, 2004), 54.
13. Ibid., 413.
14. Islam Portal, accessed March 10, 2015, http://islam.ru/en/content/story/golden-rule-islam.
15. Ibid.
16. Neusner and Chilton, *The Golden Rule*, 99–115.
17. Thomas Emil Homerin, "The Golden Rule in Islam," in Neusner and Chilton, *The Golden Rule*, 114.
18. Ibid., 115.
19. "A Common Word between Us," accessed March 15, 2015, www.acommon-word.com/the-acw-document.
20. The best example of this is the work of Scarboro Missions; see www.scarboromissions.ca.

5. What Have We Learned? Is God Necessary for Morality?

1. Slavoj Zizek, "If There Is a God, Then Anything Is Permitted," Australian Broadcasting Company, *Religion and Ethics* (television show), April 17, 2012, abc.net.au.
2. Michael Shermer, *The Science of Good and Evil* (New York: Henry Holt, 2004), 153.
3. Ibid.
4. Ibid., 154.

6. What's Love Got to Do with It? The Golden Rule and Reciprocity

1. William Scott Green, "Parsing Reciprocity: Questions for the Golden Rule," in *The Golden Rule: Analytical Perspectives*, ed. Jacob Neusner and Bruce Chilton (Lanham, MD: University Press of America, 2009), 2.
2. Bernard Gert, "Morality versus Slogans," in Neusner and Chilton, *The Golden Rule*, 3.
3. Robert Kurzman, "Biological Foundations of Reciprocity," in *Trust and Reciprocity: Interdisciplinary Lessons from Experimental Research*, ed. Elinor Ostrom and James Walker (New York: Russell Sage Foundation, 2003), 112.
4. Ibid., 112.
5. Lawrence Becker, *Reciprocity* (Chicago: University of Chicago Press, 1990), 3.
6. Ibid., 81.
7. Ibid., 79.
8. Lenn Goodman, *Love Thy Neighbor as Thyself* (New York: Oxford University Press, 2008), 14.

7. Who Am I? The Golden Rule and the Nature of Self

1. Aristotle, *Politics* 1.1253a (New York: Penguin Classics, 1981), 59, adapted. I chose a different translation to give you a sense of the range of Aristotle's original Greek text.
2. Rollo May, *Existence: A New Dimension in Psychiatry and Psychology* (New York: Basic Books, 1958), 12.
3. Jean-Paul Sartre, *Existentialism Is a Humanism* (New Haven: Yale University Press, 2007), 22, 37.
4. May, *Existence*, 12.
5. Rollo May, *Existential Psychology* (New York: Random House, 1960), 14.
6. Daniel C. Dennett, *Freedom Evolves* (New York: Viking, 2003), 273.
7. Ibid., 274.
8. Thomas Aquinas, *The Summa Theologica*, Supplementum Tertia Partis, question 94, article 1.
9. Alan Watts, *The Book: On the Taboo against Knowing Who You Are* (New York: Random House, 1989).
10. Dr. Gazzanga's research is explored in some detail in Ray Kurzweil, *How to Create a Mind* (New York: Viking, 2012), 226ff.
11. Kurzweil, *How to Create a Mind*, 229.
12. V. S. Ramachandran, *The Tell-Tale Brain* (New York: W.W. Norton, 2011), 247–248.
13. Ibid., 249.
14. Ibid.
15. Donald Pfaff, *The Neuroscience of Fair Play: Why We (Usually) Follow the Golden Rule* (New York: Dana Press, 2007), 16.
16. E. O. Wilson, cited in Pfaff, *The Neuroscience of Fair Play*, 16.
17. For more information, see Pfaff, *The Neuroscience of Fair Play*, 16.
18. Ibid., 62.
19. Ibid.
20. Ibid., 75.
21. Ibid., 76.
22. Ibid., 99–100.
23. Cited in Pfaff, *The Neuroscience of Fair Play*, 106.
24. Pfaff, *The Neuroscience of Fair Play*, 110.
25. Ibid., 112.
26. Ibid., 118.
27. Ibid., 121–122.
28. Brian Skyrms, *Evolution of the Social Contract* (Cambridge: Cambridge University Press, 1996), 3ff.
29. Dennett, *Freedom Evolves*, 268.

8. To Do or Not to Do: The Golden Rule and Free Agency

1. Lawrence Kohlberg, *The Philosophy of Moral Development: Moral States and the Idea of Justice* (San Francisco: Harper & Row, 1981), 17–20.
2. Carol Gilligan, *In a Different Voice: Psychological Theory and Women's Development* (Cambridge, MA: Harvard University Press, 1982), 5–23.

3. Philip Zimbardo, *The Lucifer Effect: Understanding How Good People Turn Evil* (New York: Random House, 2007), 19–21; 23–256.

4. Heidi Ravven, *The Self beyond Itself* (New York: New Press, 2013), 69.

5. Ibid., 78.

6. Ibid., 94.

7. Ibid., 136.

8. Saint Augustine, *On Genesis* (Hyde Park, NY: New City Press, 2004), 371.

9. Saint Augustine, *City of God* (New York: Cambridge University Press, 1998), 502.

10. Moses Maimonides, *Mishneh Torah, Hilchot Teshuvah* 5:5 (Brooklyn: Moznaim, 1990).

11. Ravven, *The Self Beyond Itself*, 416.

12. Ibid., 417.

9. Living the Rule: Toward a Global Ethic

1. Alan Watts, *The Book: On the Taboo against Knowing Who You Are* (New York: Random House, 1989), 88–89.

2. Ibid., 89.

3. David Bohm, *Quantum Theory* (New Jersey: Prentice-Hall, 1958), 162.

4. Joshua Greene, *Moral Tribes: Emotion, Reason, and the Gap Between Us and Them* (New York: Penguin Press, 2013), 352.

5. Hans Küng, *A Global Ethic: The Declaration of the Parliament of the World's Religions* (New York: Continuum, 1993), 23.

6. Ibid., 24.

7. Ibid., 14.

8. Ibid.

9. Ibid., 15.

10. W. E. H. Lecky, *The History of European Morals* (Los Angeles: Library of Alexandria, 2013), 100.

11. Peter Singer, *The Expanding Circle: Ethics, Evolution, and Moral Progress* (Princeton, NJ: Princeton University Press, 2011), 157.

12. Sigmund Freud, *Civilization and Its Discontents* (New York: W.W. Norton, 2010), 91–92.

13. Ibid., 92–93.

14. Ibid., 146.

15. Ibid., 146.

16. Heinrich Heine, *Gedanken und Einfalle* [section 1], cited in Freud, *Civilization and Its Discontents*, 93.

17. Slavoj Zizek, *The Neighbor* (Chicago: University of Chicago Press, 2005), 138.

18. Desmond Tutu, *No Future without Forgiveness* (New York: Image Doubleday, 1999), 31.

19. Michael Battle, *Unbuntu: I in You and You in Me* (New York: Seabury Books, 2009), 8.

20. Jala al-Din Rumi, *The Essential Rumi*, trans. Coleman Barks (New York: HarperCollins, 1996), 32.

21. Desmund Tutu, quoted in Michael Battle, *Reconciliation: The Ubuntu Theology of Desmond Tutu* (Cleveland: Pilgrim Press, 1997), 39.

22. Menachem Mendel, quoted in Rami Shapiro, *Minyan: Ten Principles for Living a Life of Integrity* (New York: Bell Tower, 1997), 42.

23. Michael Onyebuchi Eze, *Intellectual History in Contemporary South Africa* (New York: Palgrave Macmillan, 2010), 190–191.

24. Bob Nelson, *Ubuntu!* (New York: Broadway Books, 2010), 2.

25. Battle, *Reconciliation*, 49.

10. Play Different: Shifting the Game

1. Robert Wright, *The Evolution of God* (New York: Back Bay Books, 2010), 410.

2. Ibid., 413.

Bibliography and Suggestions for Further Reading

Adler, Gerhard. *The Living Symbol: A Case Study in the Process of Individuation*. New York: Pantheon Books, 1961.

Alexander, P. "Jesus and the Golden Rule." In *Hillel and Jesus: Comparative Studies of Two Major Religious Leaders*, edited by James H. Charlesworth and Loren L. Johns, 365–388. Minneapolis: Fortress Press, 1997.

————. "Jesus and the Golden Rule." In *The Historical Jesus in Recent Research*, edited by James Dunn and Scott McKnight, 489–508. Winona Lake, IN: Eisenbrauns, 2005.

Al-Qur'an: A Contemporary Translation. Translated by Ahmed Ali. Princeton, NJ: Princeton University Press, 2001.

Ali, Hafiz Abdullah Yusuf. *Three Translations of the Koran (Al-Qur'an) Side-by-Side*. Bennington, NH: Flying Chipmunk, 2009.

Armstrong, Karen. *The Great Transformation: The Beginning of Our Religious Traditions*. New York: Alfred A. Knopf, 2006.

————. *A History of God: The 4,000-Year Quest of Judaism, Christianity and Islam*. New York: Ballantine Books, 1994.

————. *Islam: A Short History*. New York: Modern Library, 2002.

————. *Muhammad: A Prophet for Our Time*. New York: HarperOne, 2007.

————. *Twelve Steps to a Compassionate Life*. New York: Anchor, 2011.

Augustine. *The City of God against the Pagans*. Edited by R. W. Dyson. New York: Cambridge University Press, 1998.

————. *On Genesis*. Edited by Boniface Ramsey. Hyde Park, NY: New City Press, 2004.

Avot de Rabbi Nathan. Translated by Judah Goldin. New Haven: Yale University Press, 1955.

Baggini, Julian. *The Ego Trick*. London: Granta Books, 2012.

Bahá'u'lláh. *The Summons of the Lord of Hosts*. Chicago: Baha'i Publishing, 2006.

Balaguer, Mark. *Free Will as an Open Scientific Problem*. Cambridge, MA: MIT Press, 2012.

Barnstone, Willis. *The Other Bible.* San Francisco: HarperSanFrancisco, 2005.

Battle, Michael. *Reconciliation: The Ubuntu Theology of Desmond Tutu.* Cleveland: Pilgrim Press, 1997.

———. *Ubuntu: I in You and You in Me.* New York: Seabury Books, 2009.

Becker, Lawrence. *Reciprocity.* Chicago: University of Chicago Press, 1990.

Becking, Bob, and Margo C. A. Korpel, eds. *The Crisis of Israelite Religion: Transformations and Religious Tradition in Exilic and Post-Exilic Times.* Leiden: Brill, 1999.

Belkin, Samuel. *In His Image: The Jewish Philosophy of Man as Expressed in Rabbinic Tradition.* London: Greenwood, 1979.

Bennet, E. A. *What Jung Really Said.* New York: Schocken Books, 1995.

Benson, Herbert. *The Relaxation Response.* New York: HarperTorch, 2000.

Berne, Eric. *Games People Play: The Basic Handbook of Transactional Analysis.* New York: Ballantine Books, 1996.

———. *Transactional Analysis in Psychotherapy: A Systematic Individual and Social Psychiatry.* Eastford, CT: Martino Fine Books, 2015.

———. *What Do You Say after You Say Hello?* New York: Bantam Books, 1973.

Bialik, Hayyim Nahman, and Yehoshua Hana Ravnitzky, eds. *The Book of Legends: Legends from the Talmud and Midrash.* New York: Schocken Books, 1992.

Bin Laden, Osama. *Messages to the World: The Statements of Osama bin Laden.* Edited by Bruce Lawrence. Brooklyn: Verso Books, 2005.

Binmore, Ken. *Game Theory and the Social Contract.* Vol. 1, *Playing Fair.* Cambridge, MA: MIT Press, 2000.

Blackburn, Simon. *Ethics: A Very Short Introduction.* New York: Oxford University Press, 2009.

Bloom, Alfred, ed. *The Essential Shinran: A Buddhist Path of True Entrusting.* Bloomington, IN: World Wisdom, 2007.

Bodhi, Bhikku. *The Numerical Discourses of the Buddha: A Translation of the Anguttara Nikaya.* Boston: Wisdom Publications, 2012.

Bohm, David. *Quantum Theory.* Mineola, NY: Dover Publications, 1989.

Bok, Sissela. *Common Values.* Kansas City: University of Missouri, 2002.

Boyce, Mary. *History of Zoroastrianism.* Vol. 1, *The Early Period.* Leiden, Neth.: Brill, 1996.

———. *History of Zoroastrianism.* Vol. 2, *Under the Archaemenians.* Leiden, Neth.: Brill, 1982.

Braithwaite, Richard Bevan. *Theory of Games as a Tool for the Moral Philosopher.* Cambridge: Cambridge University Press, 2009.

Brennan, Bernard. *The Ethics of William James.* New York: Bookman Associates, 1962.

Carse, James P. *Finite and Infinite Games: A Vision of Life as Play and Possibility.* New York: Free Press, 1986.

———. *The Religious Case against Belief*. New York: Penguin, 2009.

Cathcart, Thomas. *The Trolley Problem, or Would You Throw a Fat Guy Off a Bridge?: A Philosophical Conundrum*. New York: Workman Publishing, 2013.

Chalmers, Lord. *Buddha's Teachings, Being the Sutta Nipata or Discourse Collection*. Whitefish, MT: Literary Licensing LLC, 2011.

Churchland, Patricia S. *Braintrust: What Neuroscience Tells Us about Morality*. Princeton, NJ: Princeton University Press, 2012.

———. *Touching a Nerve: The Self as Brain*. New York: W.W. Norton, 2013.

Cohen, A. *Everyman's Talmud*. New York: Schocken Books, 1975.

Confucius. *The Analects*. Translated by David Hinton. Washington, DC: Counterpoint, 1998.

Conze, Edward. *Buddhism: Its Essence and Development*. Mineola, NY: Dover Publications, 2003.

———. *A Short History of Buddhism*. Oxford: Oneworld, 1980.

Creel, H. G. *Confucius: The Man and the Myth*. London: Kessinger, 1951.

———. *The Origins of Statecraft in China*. Chicago: University of Chicago Press, 1970.

Dalai Lama. *Beyond Religion: Ethics for a Whole World*. Boston: Mariner, 2012.

Darwin, Charles. *The Descent of Man*. North Charleston, SC: CreateSpace, 2014.

Das, Bhagavan. *Essential Unity of All Religions*. Whitefish, MT: Kessinger, 1994.

Dawson, Raymond. *The Analects*. Oxford, UK: Oxford Paperbacks, 2008.

Dennett, Daniel C. *Breaking the Spell: Religion as a Natural Phenomenon*. New York: Penguin, 2007.

———. *Elbow Room: The Varieties of Free Will Worth Wanting*. Cambridge: MIT Press, 2015.

———. *Freedom Evolves*. New York: Penguin, 2004.

Durckheim, Karlfried Graf. *The Way of Transformation: Daily Life as Spiritual Practice*. Sandpoint, ID: Morning Light Press, 2006.

Edgerton, Franklin. *The Beginnings of Indian Philosophy: Selections from the Rig Veda, Atharva Veda, Upanishads, and Mahabharata*. Cambridge, MA: Harvard University Press, 1965.

Edmunds, David. *Would You Kill the Fat Man?: The Trolley Problem and What Your Answer Tells Us about Right and Wrong*. Princeton, NJ: Princeton University Press, 2015.

Effendi, Shoghi. *God Passes By*. North Charleston, SC: CreateSpace, 2015.

Eisenstadt, S. N. *The Origins and Diversity of Axial Age Civilizations*. Albany: State University of New York Press, 1986.

Eze, Michael Onyebuchi. *Intellectual History in Contemporary South Africa*. New York: Palgrave Macmillan, 2010.

Fischer, Louis. *Gandhi and Stalin*. London: Victor Gollancz, 1948.

———. *The Life of Mahatma Ghandi*. New York: HarperCollins, 2004.

Francis of Assisi. *The Little Flowers of St. Francis*. Translated by Dom Roger Hudleston. Whitefish, MT: Kessinger, 2003.

Frankfort, Henri. *Before Philosophy: The Intellectual Adventure of Ancient Man*. New York: Penguin, 1960.

Freedman, Russell. *Confucius: The Golden Rule*. New York: Arthur A. Levine Books, 2002.

Freud, Sigmund. *Civilization and Its Discontents*. New York: W.W. Norton, 2010.

Fromm, Erich. *On Being Human*. New York: Bloomsbury Academic, 1997.

Fronsdal, Gil. *The Dhammapada: A New Translation of the Buddhist Classic with Annotations*. Boston: Shambhala, 2006.

Gardner, Howard. *Multiple Intelligences: New Horizons in Theory and Practice*. New York: Basic Books, 2006.

Gensler, Harry. *Ethics and the Golden Rule*. New York: Routledge, 2013.

Gilligan, Carol. *In a Different Voice: Psychological Theory and Women's Development*. Cambridge, MA: Harvard University Press, 2009.

Glasser, William. *Choice Theory: A New Psychology of Personal Freedom*. New York: HarperCollins, 1999.

Goodman, Lenn. *Love Thy Neighbor as Thyself*. New York: Oxford University Press, 2008.

Greene, Joshua. *Moral Tribes: Emotion, Reason, and the Gap between Us and Them*. New York: Penguin, 2014.

Haidt, Jonathan. *The Righteous Mind: Why Good People Are Divided by Politics and Religion*. New York: Vintage, 2013.

Hamilton, Sue. *Indian Philosophy: A Very Short Introduction*. New York: Oxford University Press, 2001.

Hanh, Thich Nhat. *For a Future to Be Possible: Buddhist Ethics for Everyday Life*. Berkeley, CA: Parallax Press, 2007.

———. *The Heart of the Buddha's Teaching: Transforming Suffering into Peace, Joy, and Liberation*. New York: Broadway Books, 1999.

Heisig, James W. *Imago Dei: A Study of C. G. Jung's Psychology of Religion*. Lewisburg, PA: Bucknell University Press, 1979.

Henrich, Natalie, and Joseph Henrich. *Why Humans Cooperate: A Cultural and Evolutionary Explanation*. New York: Oxford University Press, 2007.

Hillman, James. *Archetypal Psychology*. Dallas: Spring Publications, 1988.

Hirsch, Samson Raphael. *The Hirsch Chumash*. Vol. 3. Translated by Daniel Haberman. New York: Feldheim, 2005.

Hopkins, Thomas J. *The Hindu Religious Tradition*. Belmont, CA: Wadsworth, 1971.

Horne, Charles F., trans. *The Sacred Books and Early Literature of the East*. Vol. 7, *Ancient Persia*. Whitefish, MT: Kessinger, 1997.

Ireland, John. *The Udana Inspired Utterances of the Buddha*. Kandy, Sri Lanka: Buddhist Publication Society, 1990.

Ivanhoe, Philip J. *Confucian Moral Self-Cultivation*. Indianapolis: Hackett Publishing, 2000.

————. *Ethics in Confucian Tradition: The Thought of Mengzi and Wang Yangming*. Indianapolis: Hackett, 2002.

James, William. *The Varieties of Religious Experience*. Rockville, MD: Arc Manor, 2008.

Jerryson, Michael, ed. *Buddhist Warfare*. New York: Oxford University Press, 2010.

Jones, Lindsay, ed. *Encyclopedia of Religion*. New York: Thomson Gale, 2005.

Juergensmeyer, Mark. *The Oxford Handbook of Religion and Violence*. New York: Oxford University Press, 2012.

Jung, Carl G. *Modern Man in Search of a Soul*. New York: Harcourt Harvest, 1955.

Kant, Immanuel. *Groundwork of the Metaphysics of Morals*. Translated by Mary Gregor. Cambridge: Cambridge University Press, 2012.

Keown, Damien. *Buddhist Ethics: A Very Short Introduction*. New York: Oxford University Press, 2005.

Khalsa, Singh Sahib Sant Singh. *Siri Guru Granth Sahib*. Tucson: Hand Made Books, n.d.

Kidder, Rushworth. *How Good People Make Tough Choices: Resolving the Dilemmas of Ethical Living*. New York: Harper Perennial, 2009.

Kierkegaard, Søren. *Fear and Trembling*. London: Penguin Books, 1986.

Knott, Kim. *Hinduism: A Very Short Introduction*. New York: Oxford University Press, 2000.

Kohlberg, Lawrence. *The Philosophy of Moral Development: Moral Stages and the Idea of Justice*. San Francisco: Harper & Row, 1981.

————. *The Psychology of Moral Development: The Nature and Validity of Moral Stages*. San Francisco: Harper & Row, 1984.

Krich, Gregg. *Naikan: Gratitude, Grace, and the Japanese Art of Self-Reflection*. Berkeley: Stone Bridge Press, 2002.

Krishnamurti, J. *As One Is: To Free the Mind from All Conditioning*. Chino Valley, AZ: Hohm Press, 2015.

Kuhn, Harold. *Lectures on the Theory of Games*. Princeton, NJ: Princeton University Press, 2009.

Küng, Hans. *A Global Ethic: The Declaration of the Parliament of the World's Religions*. New York: Continuum, 1993.

————. *Global Responsibility: In Search of a New World Ethic*. Eugene, OR: Wipf & Stock, 2004.

————. *Yes to a Global Ethic*. New York: Continuum, 1996.

Küng, Hans, and Walter Homolka. *How to Do God and Avoid Evil: A Global Ethic from the Sources of Judaism.* Woodstock, VT: SkyLight Paths, 2009.

Kurzweil, Ray. *How to Create a Mind: The Secret of Human Thought Revealed.* New York: Penguin, 2013.

Lecky, W. E. H. *The History of European Morals from Augustus to Charlemagne.* Los Angeles: Library of Alexandria, 2009.

Lewis, Bernard. *Islam: The Religion and the People.* Upper Saddle River, NJ. FT Press, 2008.

Lobel, Diana. *The Quest for God and the Good: World Philosophy as a Living Experience.* New York: Columbia University Press, 2011.

Locke, John. *An Essay Concerning Human Understanding.* Cambridge: Hackett Publishing, 1996.

Long, D. Stephen. *Christian Ethics: A Very Short Introduction.* New York: Oxford University Press, 2010.

Lopez, Donald S. *The Story of Buddhism: A Concise Guide to Its History and Teachings.* New York: HarperOne, 2009.

Luther, Martin. *On the Jews and Their Lies.* Translated by Domenico d'Abrruzo. Princeton, NJ: Eulenspiegel Press, 2015.

Maden, Dhankishah Meherjibhai. *The Complete Text of the Pahlavi Dinkard.* Bombay: Society for the Promotion of Researches into the Zoroastrain Religion, 1911.

Magesa, Laurenti. *What Is Not Sacred? African Spirituality.* Maryknoll, NY: Orbis Books, 2013.

Maimonides, Moses. *The Guide of the Perplexed.* Vols. 1 and 2. Translated by Shlomo Pines. Chicago: University of Chicago Press, 1974.

———. *Mishneh Torah, Hilchot Teshuvah.* Brooklyn: Moznaim, 1990.

Mascaro, Juan. *The Dhammapada: The Path of Perfection.* London: Penguin Books, 1973.

May, Rollo. *Existence.* New York: Jason Aronson, 1994.

———. *Existence: A New Dimension in Psychiatry and Psychology.* New York: Basic Books, 1958.

———. *Existential Psychology.* New York: Random House, 1960.

Menninger, Karl. *Love against Hate.* New York: Harcourt Brace Jovanovich, 1970.

Mero, Laszlo. *Moral Calculations: Game Theory, Logic, and Human Frailty.* New York: Springer-Verlag, 1998.

Midgley, Mary. *The Ethical Primate: Humans, Freedom and Morality.* New York: Routledge, 1994.

———. *The Solitary Self: Darwin and the Selfish Gene.* New York: Routledge, 2014.

Miller, Jeanine. *Vision of Cosmic Order in the Vedas.* London: Routledge & Kegan Paul, 1985.

Miller, John. *God's Breath: Sacred Scriptures of the World.* New York: Marlowe, 1996.

———. *God's Light: The Prophets of the World's Great Religions.* New York: Marlowe, 2003.

Miller, Timothy. *How to Want What You Have.* New York: Harper Perennial, 2006.

Mitchell, Stephen. *Tao Te Ching: A New English Version.* Translated by Stephen Mitchell. New York: Harper Perennial, 2006.

Moffitt, Phillip. *Emotional Chaos to Clarity: Move from the Chaos of the Reactive Mind to the Clarity of the Responsive Mind.* New York: Plume, 2013.

Morgan, Diane. *Essential Islam: A Comprehensive Guide to Belief and Practice.* New York: Praeger, 2009.

Morris, Peter. *Introduction to Game Theory.* New York: Springer, 1994.

Muller, Max. *Pahlavi Texts: Part II.* Translated by E. W. West. New York: Cambridge University Press, 2012.

Ñaanamoli, Bhikkhu. *The Life of the Buddha: According to the Pali Canon.* Onalaska, WA: Pariyatti Publishing, 2003.

Nachmanides. *The Torah with Ramban's Commentary.* Vol. 5. Brooklyn: Mesorah, 2010.

Nelson, Bob. *Ubuntu!: An Inspiring Story about an African Tradition of Teamwork and Collaboration.* New York: Broadway Books, 2010.

Nesbitt, Eleanor. *Sikhism: A Very Short Introduction.* New York: Oxford University Press, 2005.

Neusner, Jacob, and Bruce Chilton, eds. *The Golden Rule: Analytical Perspectives.* Lanham, MD: University Press of America, 2009.

———, eds. *The Golden Rule: The Ethics of Reciprocity in World Religions.* New York: Bloomsbury Academic, 2009.

Noble, Miriam. *Golden Rules of World Religions.* Whitefish, MT: Kessinger, 2003.

Nowak, Martin. *Super Cooperators, Altruism, Evolution, and Why We Need Each Other to Succeed.* New York: Free Press, 2012.

O'Leary, Timothy. *Foucault and the Art of Ethics.* New York: Continuum, 2006.

Ostrom, Elinor, and James Walker, eds. *Trust and Reciprocity: Interdisciplinary Lessons for Experimental Research.* New York: Russell Sage Foundation, 2005.

Ott, Ludwig. *Fundamentals of Catholic Dogma.* Translated by Patrick Lynch. Charlotte, NC: TAN Books, 1992.

Pagels, Elaine. *The Origin of Satan: How Christians Demonized Jews, Pagans, and Heretics.* New York: Vintage, 1996.

Perpich, Diane. *The Ethics of Emmanuel Levinas.* Palo Alto, CA: Stanford University Press, 2008.

Pfaff, Donald. *The Neuroscience of Fair Play: Why We (Usually) Follow the Golden Rule.* New York: Dana Press, 2007.

Pigliucci, Massimo. *Answers for Aristotle: How Science and Philosophy Can Lead Us to a More Meaningful Life*. New York: Basic Books, 2012.

Pinker, Steven. *The Better Angels of Our Nature: Why Violence Has Declined*. New York: Penguin, 2012.

———. *The Blank Slate: The Modern Denial of Human Nature*. New York: Penguin Books, 2003.

Poole, Ross. *Morality and Modernity*. New York: Routledge, 1991.

Prothero, Stephen. *God Is Not One: The Eight Rival Religions That Run the World*. New York: HarperOne, 2011.

Putnam, Robert D. *American Grace: How Religion Divides and Unites Us*. New York: Simon & Schuster, 2012.

The Qur'an: A New Translation. Translated by M. A. S. Abdel Haleem. New York: Oxford University Press, 2004.

Ramachandran, V. S. *The Tell-Tale Brain: A Neuroscientist's Quest for What Makes Us Human*. New York: W.W. Norton, 2012.

Rauf, Muhammed Abdu. *Islam, Creed and Worship*. Washington, DC: Islamic Center, 1974.

Rauschenbusch, Walter. *Christianity and the Social Crisis*. Chicago: AMA Publications, 2012.

Ravven, Heidi. *The Self Beyond Itself: An Alternative History of Ethics, the New Brain Sciences, and the Myth of Free Will*. New York: New Press, 2013.

Rawls, John. *A Theory of Justice*. Cambridge, MA: Belknap Press, 2005.

Razi, Najm al-Din. *A Sufi Compendium: The Path of God's Bondsmen from Origin to Return*. Translated by Hamid Algar. Delmar, NY: Caravan Books, 1982.

Ridley, Matt. *The Rational Optimist: How Prosperity Evolves*. New York: Harper Perennial, 2011.

The Rig Veda. Translated by Wendy Doniger. New York: Penguin, 2005.

Ritter, William Emerson. *Charles Darwin and the Golden Rule*. Whitefish, MT: Literary Licensing, LLC, 2011.

Rosmarin, Aaron. *Golden Rules*. New York: Om, 1947.

Rost, H. T. D. *The Golden Rule: A Universal Ethic*. Oxford: George Ronald, 1986.

Rumi, Jala al-Din. *The Essential Rumi*. Translated by Coleman Barks. San Francisco: HarperOne, 2004.

Ruthven, Malise. *Islam: A Very Short Introduction*. New York: Oxford University Press, 2012.

Ruwart, Mary. *Healing Our World in an Age of Aggression*. Kalamazoo, MI: SunStar Press, 2003.

Sartre, Jean-Paul. *Existentialism Is a Humanism*. New Haven: Yale University Press, 2007.

Schimmel, Annemarie. *Mystical Dimensions of Islam*. Kuala Lumpur: Islamic Book Trust, 2010.

Schmidtz, David. *Elements of Justice*. New York: Cambridge University Press, 2006.

Sedlacek, Thomas. *Economics of Good and Evil: The Quest for Economic Meaning from Gilgamesh to Wall Street*. New York: Oxford University Press, 2013.

Sells, Edward. *The Faith of Islam*. North Charleston, SC: CreateSpace, 2015.

Shaked, Shaul, and Aturpat-I Emetan, eds. *The Wisdom of the Sasanian Sages (Denkard VI)*. Boulder, CO: Westview Press, 1979.

Shapiro, Rami. *Minyan: Ten Principles for Living a Life of Integrity*. New York: Bell Tower, 1997.

Shermer, Michael. *The Science of Good and Evil: Why People Cheat, Gossip, Care, Share, and Follow the Golden Rule*. New York: Henry Holt, 2004.

Shinn, Florence Scovel. *The Game of Life and How to Play It*. Camarillo, CA: DeVorss, 1978.

Sigmund, Karl. *The Calculus of Selfishness*. Princeton, NJ: Princeton University Press, 2010.

Singer, June. *Boundaries of the Soul: The Practice of Jung's Psychology*. New York: Anchor Books, 1994.

Singer, Peter. *The Expanding Circle: Ethics, Evolution, and Moral Progress*. Princeton, NJ: Princeton University Press, 2011.

Singh, Nagendra Kumar. *Encyclopedia of Hinduism*. New Delhi: Crescent, 2007.

Skyrms, Brian. *Evolution of the Social Contract*. Cambridge: Cambridge University Press, 2014.

Smart, Ninian. *The Religious Experience of Mankind*. New York: Scribner, 1984.

Smith, Huston. *The World's Religions*. New York: HarperOne, 2009.

Smith, Jonathan Z. *Imagining Religion: From Babylon to Jonestown*. Chicago: University of Chicago Press, 1988.

Smith, Wilfred Cantwell. *Towards a World Theology: Faith and the Comparative History of Religion*. Maryknoll, NY: Orbis Books, 1990.

Spencer, Herbert. *The Principles of Biology*. Handpress Publishing, 2013.

Stahl, Saul. *A Gentle Introduction to Game Theory*. Providence, RI: American Mathematical Society, 1999.

Steindl-Rast, David. *Gratefulness, the Heart of Prayer: An Approach to Life in Fullness*. New York: Paulist Press, 1984.

Steinsaltz, Adin. *The Thirteen Petalled Rose: A Discourse on the Essence of Jewish Existence and Belief*. New York: Basic Books, 2006.

Stewart, Ian. *Eric Berne*. London: Sage Publications, 1992.

Suzuki, Daisetz T. *Buddha of Infinite Light: The Teachings of Shin Buddhism, the Japanese Way of Wisdom and Compassion*. Boston: Shambhala, 2002.

————. *Zen and Japanese Culture*. Princeton: Princeton University Press, 2010.

Taiqing, Laozi. *T'an-Shang Kan-Ying P'ien: Treatise of the Exalted One on Response and Retribution*. Translated by Daisetz T. Suzuki. North Charleston, SC: CreateSpace, 2015.

Tarnas, Richard. *The Passion of the Western Mind: Understanding the Ideas That Have Shaped Our World View*. New York: Ballantine, 1993.

Tellinger, Michael. *Ubuntu Contributionism: A Blueprint for Human Prosperity*. Waterval Boven, South Africa: Zulu Planet, 2014.

Tichi, Cecelia. *Civic Passions: Seven Who Launched Progressive America*. Chapel Hill: University of North Carolina Press, 2011.

Tillich, Paul. *Dynamics of Faith*. San Francisco: HarperOne, 2009.

Tishby, Isaiah. *The Wisdom of the Zohar: An Anthology of Texts*. London: Oxford University Press, 1991.

Tutu, Desmond. *No Future without Forgiveness*. New York: Image Doubleday, 2000.

Ullmann-Margalit, Edna. *The Emergence of Norms*. Oxford: Oxford University Press, 2015.

Unno, Teitetsu. *River of Fire, River of Water*. New York: Doubleday, 1998.

Upanishads. Translated by Valerie Roebuck. New York: Penguin, 2004.

Victoria, Brian Daizen. *Zen at War*. New York: Rowman & Littlefield, 2006.

Vivekananda, Swami. *Is Vedanta the Future Religion?* Kolkata: Advaita Ashrama, 2013.

Wang, Robin. *Images of Women in Chinese Thought and Culture: Writings from the Pre-Qin Period through the Song Dynasty*. Indianapolis: Hackett, 2003.

Wattles, Jeffrey. *The Golden Rule*. New York: Oxford University Press, 1996.

Watts, Alan. *The Book: On the Taboo against Knowing Who You Are*. New York: Random House, 1989.

Wink, Walter. *The Human Being: Jesus and the Enigma of the Son of Man*. Minneapolis: Augsberg, 2001.

Woodhead, Linda. *Christianity: A Very Short Introduction*. New York: Oxford University Press, 2005.

Wright, Robert. *The Evolution of God*. New York: Back Bay Books, 2010.

————. *The Moral Animal: Why We Are, the Way We Are—The New Science of Evolutionary Psychology*. New York: Vintage, 1995.

————. *Nonzero: The Logic of Human Destiny*. New York: Vintage, 2001.

Zandberg, Jeroen. *The Philosophy of Ubuntu and the Origins of Democracy*. Lulu.com, 2010.

Zarruq, Ahmed. *The Principles of Sufism*. Bristol, UK: Amal Press, 2008.

Zizek, Slavoj. *The Neighbor: Three Inquiries in Political Theology*. Chicago: University of Chicago Press, 2013.

Inspiration

The Golden Rule and the Games People Play
The Ultimate Strategy for a Meaning-Filled Life
By Rami Shapiro
A guidebook for living a meaning-filled life—using the strategies of game theory and the wisdom of the Golden Rule.
6 x 9, 176 pp, Quality PB, 978-1-59473-598-1 **$16.99**

Deepening Engagement
Essential Wisdom for Listening and Leading with Purpose, Meaning and Joy
By Diane M. Millis, PhD; Foreword by Rob Lehman
A toolkit for community building as well as a resource for personal growth and small group enrichment.
5 x 7¼, 176 pp, Quality PB, 978-1-59473-584-4 **$14.99**

The Rebirthing of God
Christianity's Struggle for New Beginnings
By John Philip Newell
Drawing on modern prophets from East and West, and using the holy island of Iona as an icon of new beginnings, Newell dares us to imagine a new birth from deep within Christianity, a fresh stirring of the Spirit.
6 x 9, 160 pp, HC, 978-1-59473-542-4 **$19.99**

Finding God Beyond Religion: A Guide for Skeptics, Agnostics & Unorthodox Believers Inside & Outside the Church
By Tom Stella; Foreword by The Rev. Canon Marianne Wells Borg
Reinterprets traditional religious teachings central to the Christian faith for people who have outgrown the beliefs and devotional practices that once made sense to them. 6 x 9, 160 pp, Quality PB, 978-1-59473-485-4 **$16.99**

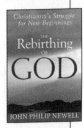

Fully Awake and Truly Alive: Spiritual Practices to Nurture Your Soul
By Rev. Jane E. Vennard; Foreword by Rami Shapiro
Illustrates the joys and frustrations of spiritual practice across religious traditions; provides exercises and meditations to help you become more fully alive.
6 x 9, 208 pp, Quality PB, 978-1-59473-473-1 **$16.99**

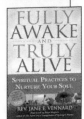

Perennial Wisdom for the Spiritually Independent
Sacred Teachings—Annotated & Explained
Annotation by Rami Shapiro; Foreword by Richard Rohr
Weaves sacred texts and teachings from the world's major religions into a coherent exploration of the five core questions at the heart of every religion's search.
5½ x 8½, 336 pp, Quality PB, 978-1-59473-515-8 **$16.99**

Journeys of Simplicity: Traveling Light with Thomas Merton, Bashō, Edward Abbey, Annie Dillard & Others *By Philip Harnden*
5 x 7¼, 144 pp, Quality PB, 978-1-59473-181-5 **$12.99**

Saving Civility: 52 Ways to Tame Rude, Crude & Attitude for a Polite Planet
By Sara Hacala 6 x 9, 240 pp, Quality PB, 978-1-59473-314-7 **$16.99**

Spiritually Healthy Divorce: Navigating Disruption with Insight & Hope
By Carolyne Call 6 x 9, 224 pp, Quality PB, 978-1-59473-288-1 **$16.99**

Judaism / Christianity / Islam / Interfaith

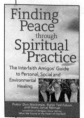

Finding Peace through Spiritual Practice
The Interfaith Amigos' Guide to Personal, Social and Environmental Healing
By Pastor Don Mackenzie, Rabbi Ted Falcon and Imam Jamal Rahman
A look at the specific issues in modern pluralistic society and the spiritual practices that can help transcend roadblocks to effective collaboration on the critical issues of today.
6 x 9, 200 pp (est), Quality PB, 978-1-59473-604-9 **$16.99**

Struggling in Good Faith
LGBTQI Inclusion from 13 American Religious Perspectives
Edited by Mychal Copeland and D'vorah Rose; Foreword by Bishop Gene Robinson
A multifaceted sourcebook telling the story of reconciliation, celebration and struggle for LGBTQI inclusion across the religious landscape in America.
6 x 9, 250 pp (est), Quality PB, 978-1-59473-602-5 **$19.99**

Practical Interfaith: How to Find Our Common Humanity as We Celebrate Diversity
By Rev. Steven Greenebaum
Explores Interfaith as a faith—and as a positive way to move forward.
6 x 9, 176 pp, Quality PB, 978-1-59473-569-1 **$16.99**

Sacred Laughter of the Sufis: Awakening the Soul with the Mulla's Comic Teaching Stories & Other Islamic Wisdom
By Imam Jamal Rahman
The legendary wisdom stories of the Mulla, Islam's great comic foil, with spiritual insights for seekers of all traditions—or none.
6 x 9, 192 pp, Quality PB, 978-1-59473-547-9 **$16.99**

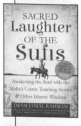

Religion Gone Astray: What We Found at the Heart of Interfaith
By Pastor Don Mackenzie, Rabbi Ted Falcon and Imam Jamal Rahman
Explores that which divides us personally, spiritually and institutionally.
6 x 9, 192 pp, Quality PB, 978-1-59473-317-8 **$18.99**

Blessed Relief: What Christians Can Learn from Buddhists about Suffering
By Gordon Peerman 6 x 9, 208 pp, Quality PB, 978-1-59473-252-2 **$16.99**

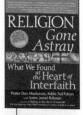

Christians & Jews—Faith to Faith: Tragic History, Promising Present, Fragile Future
By Rabbi James Rudin
6 x 9, 288 pp, HC, 978-1-58023-432-0 **$24.99**; Quality PB, 978-1-58023-717-8 **$18.99***

Getting to the Heart of Interfaith: The Eye-Opening, Hope-Filled Friendship of a Pastor, a Rabbi & an Imam
By Pastor Don Mackenzie, Rabbi Ted Falcon and Imam Jamal Rahman
6 x 9, 192 pp, Quality PB, 978-1-59473-263-8 **$16.99**

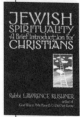

The Jewish Approach to God: A Brief Introduction for Christians
By Rabbi Neil Gillman, PhD 5½ x 8½, 192 pp, Quality PB, 978-1-58023-190-9 **$16.95***

The Jewish Approach to Repairing the World (Tikkun Olam)
A Brief Introduction for Christians *By Rabbi Elliot N. Dorff, PhD, with Rev. Cory Willson*
5½ x 8½, 256 pp, Quality PB, 978-1-58023-349-1 **$16.99***

The Jewish Connection to Israel, the Promised Land: A Brief Introduction for Christians
By Rabbi Eugene Korn, PhD 5½ x 8½, 192 pp, Quality PB, 978-1-58023-318-7 **$14.99***

Jewish Holidays: A Brief Introduction for Christians
By Rabbi Kerry M. Olitzky and Rabbi Daniel Judson 5½ x 8½, 176 pp, Quality PB, 978-1-58023-302-6 **$18.99***

Jewish Ritual: A Brief Introduction for Christians
By Rabbi Kerry M. Olitzky and Rabbi Daniel Judson 5½ x 8½, 144 pp, Quality PB, 978-1-58023-210-4 **$14.99***

Jewish Spirituality: A Brief Introduction for Christians
By Rabbi Lawrence Kushner 5½ x 8½, 112 pp, Quality PB, 978-1-58023-150-3 **$12.95***

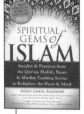

Spiritual Gems of Islam: Insights & Practices from the Qur'an, Hadith, Rumi & Muslim Teaching Stories to Enlighten the Heart & Mind
By Imam Jamal Rahman
6 x 9, 256 pp, Quality PB, 978-1-59473-430-4 **$16.99**

*A book from Jewish Lights, SkyLight Paths' sister imprint

Sacred Texts—SkyLight Illuminations Series

Offers today's spiritual seeker an enjoyable entry into the great classic texts of the world's spiritual traditions. Each classic is presented in an accessible translation, with facing pages of guided commentary from experts, giving you the keys you need to understand the history, context and meaning of the text.

CHRISTIANITY

The Book of Common Prayer: A Spiritual Treasure Chest—
Selections Annotated & Explained
Annotation by The Rev. Canon C. K. Robertson, PhD; Foreword by The Most Rev. Katharine Jefferts Schori; Preface by Archbishop Desmond Tutu
Makes available the riches of this spiritual treasure chest for all who are interested in deepening their life of prayer, building stronger relationships and making a difference in their world. 5½ x 8½, 208 pp, Quality PB, 978-1-59473-524-0 **$16.99**

Celtic Christian Spirituality: Essential Writings—Annotated & Explained
Annotation by Mary C. Earle; Foreword by John Philip Newell
Explores how the writings of this lively tradition embody the gospel.
5½ x 8½, 176 pp, Quality PB, 978-1-59473-302-4 **$16.99**

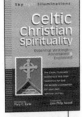

Desert Fathers and Mothers: Early Christian Wisdom Sayings—
Annotated & Explained *Annotation by Christine Valters Paintner, PhD*
Opens up wisdom of the desert fathers and mothers for readers with no previous knowledge of Western monasticism and early Christianity.
5½ x 8½, 192 pp, Quality PB, 978-1-59473-373-4 **$16.99**

The End of Days: Essential Selections from Apocalyptic Texts—
Annotated & Explained *Annotation by Robert G. Clouse, PhD*
Helps you understand the complex Christian visions of the end of the world.
5½ x 8½, 224 pp, Quality PB, 978-1-59473-170-9 **$16.99**

The Hidden Gospel of Matthew: Annotated & Explained
Translation & Annotation by Ron Miller
Discover the words and events that have the strongest connection to the historical Jesus.
5½ x 8½, 272 pp, Quality PB, 978-1-59473-038-2 **$16.99**

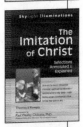

The Imitation of Christ: Selections Annotated & Explained
Annotation by Paul Wesley Chilcote, PhD; By Thomas à Kempis
Adapted from John Wesley's The Christian's Pattern
Let Jesus's example of holiness, humility and purity of heart be a companion on your own spiritual journey.
5½ x 8½, 224 pp, Quality PB, 978-1-59473-434-2 **$16.99**

The Infancy Gospels of Jesus: Apocryphal Tales from the Childhoods of Mary and Jesus—Annotated & Explained
Translation & Annotation by Stevan Davies; Foreword by A. Edward Siecienski, PhD
A startling presentation of the early lives of Mary, Jesus and other biblical figures that will amuse and surprise you. 5½ x 8½, 176 pp, Quality PB, 978-1-59473-258-4 **$16.99**

John & Charles Wesley: Selections from Their Writings and Hymns—
Annotated & Explained *Annotation by Paul W. Chilcote, PhD*
A unique presentation of the writings of these two inspiring brothers brings together some of the most essential material from their large corpus of work.
5½ x 8½, 288 pp, Quality PB, 978-1-59473-309-3 **$16.99**

Julian of Norwich: Selections from *Revelations of Divine Love*—
Annotated & Explained *Annotation by Mary C. Earle; Foreword by Roberta C. Bondi*
Addresses topics including the infinite nature of God, the life of prayer, God's suffering with us, the eternal and undying life of the soul, the motherhood of Jesus and the motherhood of God and more.
5½ x 8½, 224 pp, Quality PB, 978-1-59473-513-4 **$16.99**

Sacred Texts—continued

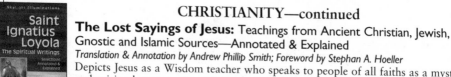

CHRISTIANITY—continued

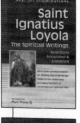

The Lost Sayings of Jesus: Teachings from Ancient Christian, Jewish, Gnostic and Islamic Sources—Annotated & Explained
Translation & Annotation by Andrew Phillip Smith; Foreword by Stephan A. Hoeller
Depicts Jesus as a Wisdom teacher who speaks to people of all faiths as a mystic and spiritual master. 5½ x 8½, 240 pp, Quality PB, 978-1-59473-172-3 **$16.99**

Philokalia: The Eastern Christian Spiritual Texts—Selections Annotated & Explained *Annotation by Allyne Smith; Translation by G. E. H. Palmer, Phillip Sherrard and Bishop Kallistos Ware* The first approachable introduction to the wisdom of the Philokalia. 5½ x 8½, 240 pp, Quality PB, 978-1-59473-103-7 **$18.99**

The Sacred Writings of Paul: Selections Annotated & Explained
Translation & Annotation by Ron Miller Leads you into the exciting immediacy of Paul's teachings. 5½ x 8½, 224 pp, Quality PB, 978-1-59473-213-3 **$16.99**

Saint Augustine of Hippo: Selections from *Confessions* and Other Essential Writings—Annotated & Explained
Annotation by Joseph T. Kelley, PhD; Translation by the Augustinian Heritage Institute
Provides insight into the mind and heart of this foundational Christian figure.
5½ x 8½, 272 pp, Quality PB, 978-1-59473-282-9 **$18.99**

Saint Ignatius Loyola—The Spiritual Writings: Selections Annotated & Explained *Annotation by Mark Mossa, SJ* Focuses on the practical mysticism of Ignatius of Loyola. 5½ x 8½, 288 pp, Quality PB, 978-1-59473-301-7 **$18.99**

Sex Texts from the Bible: Selections Annotated & Explained
Translation & Annotation by Teresa J. Hornsby; Foreword by Amy-Jill Levine
Demystifies the Bible's ideas on gender roles, marriage, sexual orientation, virginity, lust and sexual pleasure. 5½ x 8½, 208 pp, Quality PB, 978-1-59473-217-1 **$16.99**

Spiritual Writings on Mary: Annotated & Explained
Annotation by Mary Ford-Grabowsky; Foreword by Andrew Harvey
Examines the role of Mary, the mother of Jesus, as a source of inspiration in history and in life today. 5½ x 8½, 272 pp, Quality PB, 978-1-59473-001-6 **$16.99**

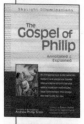

The Way of a Pilgrim: The Jesus Prayer Journey—Annotated & Explained
Translation & Annotation by Gleb Pokrovsky; Foreword by Andrew Harvey A classic of Russian Orthodox spirituality. 5½ x 8½, 160 pp, Illus., Quality PB, 978-1-893361-31-7 **$15.99**

GNOSTICISM

Gnostic Writings on the Soul: Annotated & Explained
Translation & Annotation by Andrew Phillip Smith; Foreword by Stephan A. Hoeller
Reveals the inspiring ways your soul can remember and return to its unique, divine purpose. 5½ x 8½, 144 pp, Quality PB, 978-1-59473-220-1 **$16.99**

The Gospel of Philip: Annotated & Explained
Translation & Annotation by Andrew Phillip Smith; Foreword by Stevan Davies
Reveals otherwise unrecorded sayings of Jesus and fragments of Gnostic mythology.
5½ x 8½, 160 pp, Quality PB, 978-1-59473-111-2 **$16.99**

The Gospel of Thomas: Annotated & Explained
Translation & Annotation by Stevan Davies; Foreword by Andrew Harvey
Sheds new light on the origins of Christianity and portrays Jesus as a wisdom-loving sage.
5½ x 8½, 192 pp, Quality PB, 978-1-893361-45-4 **$16.99**

The Secret Book of John: The Gnostic Gospel—Annotated & Explained
Translation & Annotation by Stevan Davies The most significant and influential text of the ancient Gnostic religion. 5½ x 8½, 208 pp, Quality PB, 978-1-59473-082-5 **$18.99**

See Inspiration for *Perennial Wisdom for the Spiritually Independent: Sacred Teachings—Annotated & Explained*

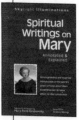
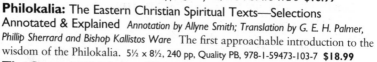

Sacred Texts—continued

JUDAISM

The Book of Job: Annotated & Explained
Translation and Annotation by Donald Kraus; Foreword by Dr. Marc Brettler
Clarifies for today's readers what Job is, how to overcome difficulties in the text, and what it may mean for us. 5½ x 8½, 256 pp, Quality PB, 978-1-59473-389-5 **$16.99**

The Divine Feminine in Biblical Wisdom Literature
Selections Annotated & Explained
Translation & Annotation by Rabbi Rami Shapiro; Foreword by Rev. Cynthia Bourgeault, PhD
Uses the Hebrew Bible and Wisdom literature to explain Sophia's way of wisdom and illustrate Her creative energy. 5½ x 8½, 240 pp, Quality PB, 978-1-59473-109-9 **$18.99**

Ecclesiastes: Annotated & Explained
Translation & Annotation by Rabbi Rami Shapiro; Foreword by Rev. Barbara Cawthorne Crafton
A timeless teaching on living well amid uncertainty and insecurity.
5½ x 8½, 160 pp, Quality PB, 978-1-59473-287-4 **$16.99**

Embracing the Divine Feminine: Finding God through the Ecstasy of Physical Love—The Song of Songs Annotated & Explained
Translation & Annotation by Rabbi Rami Shapiro; Foreword by Rev. Cynthia Bourgeault, PhD
Restores the Song of Songs' eroticism and interprets it as a celebration of the love between the Divine Feminine and the contemporary spiritual seeker.
5½ x 8½, 176 pp, Quality PB, 978-1-59473-575-2 **$16.99**

Ethics of the Sages: *Pirke Avot*—Annotated & Explained
Translation & Annotation by Rabbi Rami Shapiro Clarifies the ethical teachings of the early Rabbis. 5½ x 8½, 192 pp, Quality PB, 978-1-59473-207-2 **$16.99**

Hasidic Tales: Annotated & Explained
Translation & Annotation by Rabbi Rami Shapiro; Foreword by Andrew Harvey
Introduces the legendary tales of the impassioned Hasidic rabbis, presenting them as stories rather than as parables. 5½ x 8½, 240 pp, Quality PB, 978-1-893361-86-7 **$18.99**

The Hebrew Prophets: Selections Annotated & Explained
Translation & Annotation by Rabbi Rami Shapiro; Foreword by Rabbi Zalman M. Schachter-Shalomi (z"l)
Makes the wisdom of these timeless teachers available to readers with no previous knowledge of the prophets. 5½ x 8½, 224 pp, Quality PB, 978-1-59473-037-5 **$16.99**

Maimonides—Essential Teachings on Jewish Faith & Ethics
The Book of Knowledge & the Thirteen Principles of Faith—Annotated & Explained
Translation and Annotation by Rabbi Marc D. Angel, PhD
Opens up for us Maimonides's views on the nature of God, providence, prophecy, free will, human nature, repentance and more.
5½ x 8½, 224 pp, Quality PB, 978-1-59473-311-6 **$18.99**

Proverbs: Annotated & Explained
Translation and Annotation by Rabbi Rami Shapiro
Demonstrates how these complex poetic forms are actually straightforward instructions to live simply, without rationalizations and excuses.
5½ x 8½, 288 pp, Quality PB, 978-1-59473-310-9 **$16.99**

Tanya, the Masterpiece of Hasidic Wisdom
Selections Annotated & Explained *Translation & Annotation by Rabbi Rami Shapiro*
Foreword by Rabbi Zalman M. Schachter-Shalomi (z"l)
Clarifies one of the most powerful and potentially transformative books of Jewish wisdom. 5½ x 8½, 240 pp, Quality PB, 978-1-59473-275-1 **$18.99**

Zohar: Annotated & Explained
Translation & Annotation by Daniel C. Matt; Foreword by Andrew Harvey
The canonical text of Jewish mystical tradition.
5½ x 8½, 176 pp, Quality PB, 978-1-893361-51-5 **$18.99**

See Inspiration for *Perennial Wisdom for the Spiritually Independent: Sacred Teachings—Annotated & Explained*

Sacred Texts—continued

ISLAM

Ghazali on the Principles of Islamic Spirituality
Selections from *The Forty Foundations of Religion*—Annotated & Explained
Translation & Annotation by Aaron Spevack, PhD; Foreword by M. Fethullah Gülen
Makes the core message of this influential spiritual master relevant to anyone seeking a balanced understanding of Islam.
5½ x 8½, 336 pp, Quality PB, 978-1-59473-284-3 **$18.99**

The Qur'an and Sayings of Prophet Muhammad
Selections Annotated & Explained
Annotation by Sohaib N. Sultan; Translation by Yusuf Ali, Revised by Sohaib N. Sultan
Foreword by Jane I. Smith
Presents the foundational wisdom of Islam in an easy-to-use format.
5½ x 8½, 256 pp, Quality PB, 978-1-59473-222-5 **$16.99**

Rumi and Islam: Selections from His Stories, Poems, and Discourses—
Annotated & Explained *Translation & Annotation by Ibrahim Gamard*
Focuses on Rumi's place within the Sufi tradition of Islam, providing insight into the mystical side of the religion. 5½ x 8½, 240 pp, Quality PB, 978-1-59473-002-3 **$18.99**

See Inspiration for *Perennial Wisdom for the Spiritually Independent: Sacred Teachings—Annotated & Explained*

EASTERN RELIGIONS

The Art of War—Spirituality for Conflict: Annotated & Explained
By Sun Tzu; Annotation by Thomas Huynh; Translation by Thomas Huynh and the Editors at Sonshi.com; Foreword by Marc Benioff; Preface by Thomas Cleary
Highlights principles that encourage a perceptive and spiritual approach to conflict.
5½ x 8½, 256 pp, Quality PB, 978-1-59473-244-7 **$16.99**

Bhagavad Gita: Annotated & Explained
Translation by Shri Purohit Swami; Annotation by Kendra Crossen Burroughs
Foreword by Andrew Harvey Presents the classic text's teachings—with no previous knowledge of Hinduism required. 5½ x 8½, 192 pp, Quality PB, 978-1-893361-28-7 **$18.99**

Chuang-tzu: The Tao of Perfect Happiness—Selections Annotated & Explained
Translation & Annotation by Livia Kohn, PhD
Presents Taoism's central message of reverence for the "Way" of the natural world.
5½ x 8½, 240 pp, Quality PB, 978-1-59473-296-6 **$16.99**

Confucius, the *Analects*: The Path of the Sage—Selections Annotated
& Explained *Annotation by Rodney L. Taylor, PhD; Translation by James Legge,*
Revised by Rodney L. Taylor, PhD Explores the ethical and spiritual meaning behind the Confucian way of learning and self-cultivation.
5½ x 8½, 192 pp, Quality PB, 978-1-59473-306-2 **$16.99**

Dhammapada: Annotated & Explained
Translation by Max Müller, Revised by Jack Maguire; Annotation by Jack Maguire
Foreword by Andrew Harvey Contains all of Buddhism's key teachings, plus commentary that explains all the names, terms and references.
5½ x 8½, 160 pp, b/w photos, Quality PB, 978-1-893361-42-3 **$14.95**

Selections from the Gospel of Sri Ramakrishna: Annotated & Explained
Translation by Swami Nikhilananda; Annotation by Kendra Crossen Burroughs
Foreword by Andrew Harvey Introduces the fascinating world of the Indian mystic and the universal appeal of his message. 5½ x 8½, 240 pp, b/w photos, Quality PB, 978-1-893361-46-1 **$16.95**

Tao Te Ching: Annotated & Explained
Translation & Annotation by Derek Lin; Foreword by Lama Surya Das
Introduces an Eastern classic in an accessible, poetic and completely original way.
5½ x 8½, 208 pp, Quality PB, 978-1-59473-204-1 **$16.99**

Sacred Texts—continued

MORMONISM

The Book of Mormon: Selections Annotated & Explained
Annotation by Jana Riess; Foreword by Phyllis Tickle Explores the sacred epic that is cherished by more than twelve million members of the LDS church as the keystone of their faith. 5½ x 8½ , 272 pp, Quality PB, 978-1-59473-076-4 **$16.99**

NATIVE AMERICAN

Native American Stories of the Sacred: Annotated & Explained
Retold & Annotated by Evan T. Pritchard These teaching tales contain elegantly simple illustrations of time-honored truths. 5½ x 8½, 272 pp, Quality PB, 978-1-59473-112-9 **$18.99**

STOICISM

The Meditations of Marcus Aurelius: Selections Annotated & Explained
Annotation by Russell McNeil, PhD; Translation by George Long, Revised by Russell McNeil, PhD Ancient Stoic wisdom that speaks vibrantly today about life, business, government and spirit. 5½ x 8½, 288 pp, Quality PB, 978-1-59473-236-2 **$16.99**

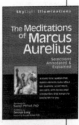

Hinduism / Vedanta

The Four Yogas: A Guide to the Spiritual Paths of Action, Devotion,
Meditation and Knowledge *By Swami Adiswarananda*
6 x 9, 320 pp, Quality PB, 978-1-59473-223-2 **$19.99**

Meditation & Its Practices: A Definitive Guide to Techniques and Traditions of
Meditation in Yoga and Vedanta *By Swami Adiswarananda*
6 x 9, 504 pp, Quality PB, 978-1-59473-105-1 **$24.99**

The Spiritual Quest and the Way of Yoga: The Goal, the Journey and the Milestones
By Swami Adiswarananda 6 x 9, 288 pp, HC, 978-1-59473-113-6 **$29.99**

Sri Ramakrishna, the Face of Silence *By Swami Nikhilananda
and Dhan Gopal Mukerji; Edited and with an Introduction by Swami Adiswarananda
Foreword by Dhan Gopal Mukerji II* 6 x 9, 352 pp, Quality PB, 978-1-59473-233-1 **$21.99**

The Vedanta Way to Peace and Happiness *By Swami Adiswarananda*
6 x 9, 240 pp, Quality PB, 978-1-59473-180-8 **$18.99**

Vivekananda, World Teacher: His Teachings on the Spiritual Unity of Humankind
Edited and with an Introduction by Swami Adiswarananda
6 x 9, 272 pp, Quality PB, 978-1-59473-210-2 **$21.99**

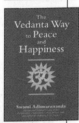

Sikhism

The First Sikh Spiritual Master: Timeless Wisdom from the Life and Teachings of
Guru Nanak *By Harish Dhillon* 6 x 9, 192 pp, Quality PB, 978-1-59473-209-6 **$18.99**

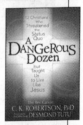

Spiritual Biography

A Dangerous Dozen: Twelve Christians Who Threatened the Status
Quo but Taught Us to Live Like Jesus
By The Rev. Canon C. K. Robertson, PhD; Foreword by Archbishop Desmond Tutu
Profiles twelve visionary men and women who challenged society and showed the world a different way of living. 6 x 9, 208 pp, Quality PB, 978-1-59473-298-0 **$16.99**

Mahatma Gandhi: His Life and Ideas *By Charles F. Andrews; Foreword by Dr. Arun Gandhi*
Examines the religious ideas and political dynamics that influenced the birth of the peaceful resistance movement. 6 x 9, 336 pp, b/w photos, Quality PB, 978-1-893361-89-8 **$18.95**

Bede Griffiths: An Introduction to His Interspiritual Thought
By Wayne Teasdale Explores the intersection of Hinduism and Christianity.
6 x 9, 288 pp, Quality PB, 978-1-893361-77-5 **$18.95**

Spiritual Leaders Who Changed the World: The Essential Handbook to the
Past Century of Religion *Edited by Ira Rifkin and the Editors at SkyLight Paths
Foreword by Dr. Robert Coles* 6 x 9, 304 pp, b/w photos, Quality PB, 978-1-59473-241-6 **$18.99**

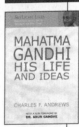

Children's Spiritual Biography

MULTICULTURAL, NONDENOMINATIONAL, NONSECTARIAN

Ten Amazing People
And How They Changed the World
By Maura D. Shaw; Foreword by Dr. Robert Coles
Full-color illus. by Stephen Marchesi

For ages 7 & up

Shows kids that spiritual people can have an exciting impact on the world around them. Kids will delight in reading about these amazing people and what they accomplished through their words and actions.

Black Elk • Dorothy Day • Malcolm X • Mahatma Gandhi • Martin Luther King, Jr. • Mother Teresa • Janusz Korczak • Desmond Tutu • Thich Nhat Hanh • Albert Schweitzer

"Best Juvenile/Young Adult Non-Fiction Book of the Year."
—*Independent Publisher*

"Will inspire adults and children alike."
—*Globe and Mail* (Toronto)

8½ x 11, 48 pp, Full-color illus., HC, 978-1-893361-47-8 **$18.99** For ages 7 & up

Spiritual Biographies for Young People
For Ages 7 & Up

By Maura D. Shaw; Illus. by Stephen Marchesi
6¾ x 8¾, 32 pp, Full-color and b/w illus., HC

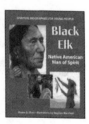 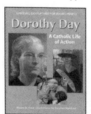 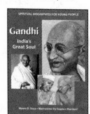 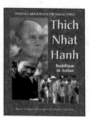

Black Elk: Native American Man of Spirit
Through historically accurate illustrations and photos, inspiring age-appropriate activities and Black Elk's own words, this colorful biography introduces children to a remarkable person who ensured that the traditions and beliefs of his people would not be forgotten.
978-1-59473-043-6 **$12.99**

Dorothy Day: A Catholic Life of Action
Introduces children to one of the most inspiring women of the twentieth century, a down-to-earth spiritual leader who saw the presence of God in every person she met. Includes practical activities, a timeline and a list of important words to know.
978-1-59473-011-5 **$12.99**

Gandhi: India's Great Soul
The only biography of Gandhi that balances a simple text with illustrations, photos and activities that encourage children and adults to talk about how to make changes happen without violence. Introduces children to important concepts of freedom, equality and justice among people of all backgrounds and religions.
978-1-893361-91-1 **$12.95**

Thich Nhat Hanh: Buddhism in Action
Warm illustrations, photos, age-appropriate activities and Thich Nhat Hanh's own poems introduce a great man to children in a way they can understand and enjoy. Includes a list of important Buddhist words to know.
978-1-893361-87-4 **$12.95**

Retirement and Later-Life Spirituality

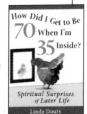

Caresharing
A Reciprocal Approach to Caregiving and Care Receiving in the Complexities of Aging, Illness or Disability
By Marty Richards

Shows how to move from independent to *inter*dependent caregiving, so that the "cared for" and the "carer" share a deep sense of connection.

6 x 9, 256 pp, Quality PB, 978-1-59473-286-7 **$16.99**; HC, 978-1-59473-247-8 **$24.99**

How Did I Get to Be 70 When I'm 35 Inside?
Spiritual Surprises of Later Life
By Linda Douty

Encourages you to focus on the inner changes of aging to help you greet your later years as the grand adventure they can be.

6 x 9, 208 pp, Quality PB, 978-1-59473-297-3 **$16.99**

Soul Fire
Accessing Your Creativity
By Thomas Ryan, CSP

This inspiring guide shows you how to cultivate your creative spirit, particularly in the second half of life, as a way to encourage personal growth, enrich your spiritual life and deepen your communion with God.

6 x 9, 160 pp, Quality PB, 978-1-59473-243-0 **$16.99**

Restoring Life's Missing Pieces
The Spiritual Power of Remembering & Reuniting with People, Places, Things & Self
By Caren Goldman; Foreword by Dr. Nancy Copeland-Payton

Delve deeply into ways that your body, mind and spirit answer the Spirit of Re-union's calls to reconnect with people, places, things and self. A powerful and thought-provoking look at "reunions" of all kinds as roads to remembering the missing pieces of our stories, psyches and souls.

6 x 9, 208 pp, Quality PB, 978-1-59473-295-9 **$16.99**

Creative Aging
Rethinking Retirement and Non-Retirement in a Changing World
By Marjory Zoet Bankson

Explores the spiritual dimensions of retirement and aging and offers creative ways for you to share your gifts and experience, particularly when retirement leaves you questioning who you are when you are no longer defined by your career.

6 x 9, 160 pp, Quality PB, 978-1-59473-281-2 **$16.99**

Creating a Spiritual Retirement
A Guide to the Unseen Possibilities in Our Lives
By Molly Srode

Retirement can be an opportunity to refocus on your soul and deepen the presence of spirit in your life. With fresh spiritual reflections and questions to help you explore this new phase.

6 x 9, 208 pp, b/w photos, Quality PB, 978-1-59473-050-4 **$14.99**

Keeping Spiritual Balance as We Grow Older
More than 65 Creative Ways to Use Purpose, Prayer, and the Power of Spirit to Build a Meaningful Retirement
By Molly and Bernie Srode

As we face new demands on our bodies, it's easy to focus on the physical and forget about the transformations in our spiritual selves. This book is brimming with creative, practical ideas to add purpose and spirit to a meaningful retirement.

8 x 8, 224 pp, Quality PB, 978-1-59473-042-9 **$16.99**

Spiritual Practice—The Sacred Art of Living Series

Teaching—The Sacred Art: The Joy of Opening Minds & Hearts
By Rev. Jane E. Vennard Explores the elements that make teaching a sacred art, recognizing it as a call to service rather than a job, and a vocation rather than a profession. 5½ x 8½, 160 pp, Quality PB, 978-1-59473-585-1 **$16.99**

Conversation—The Sacred Art: Practicing Presence in an Age of Distraction
By Diane M. Millis, PhD; Foreword by Rev. Tilden Edwards, PhD
5½ x 8½, 192 pp, Quality PB, 978-1-59473-474-8 **$16.99**

Dance—The Sacred Art: The Joy of Movement as a Spiritual Practice
By Cynthia Winton-Henry 5½ x 8½, 224 pp, Quality PB, 978-1-59473-268-3 **$16.99**

Dreaming—The Sacred Art: Incubating, Navigating & Interpreting Sacred Dreams for Spiritual & Personal Growth *By Lori Joan Swick, PhD*
5½ x 8½, 224 pp, Quality PB, 978-1-59473-544-8 **$16.99**

Fly-Fishing—The Sacred Art: Casting a Fly as a Spiritual Practice
By Rabbi Eric Eisenkramer and Rev. Michael Attas, MD; Foreword by Chris Wood, CEO, Trout Unlimited; Preface by Lori Simon, executive director, Casting for Recovery
5½ x 8½, 160 pp, Quality PB, 978-1-59473-299-7 **$16.99**

Giving—The Sacred Art: Creating a Lifestyle of Generosity
By Lauren Tyler Wright 5½ x 8½, 208 pp, Quality PB, 978-1-59473-224-9 **$16.99**

Haiku—The Sacred Art: A Spiritual Practice in Three Lines
By Margaret D. McGee 5½ x 8½, 192 pp, Quality PB, 978-1-59473-269-0 **$16.99**

Hospitality—The Sacred Art: Discovering the Hidden Spiritual Power of Invitation and Welcome *By Rev. Nanette Sawyer; Foreword by Rev. Dirk Ficca*
5½ x 8½, 208 pp, Quality PB, 978-1-59473-228-7 **$16.99**

Labyrinths from the Outside In, 2nd Edition
Walking to Spiritual Insight—A Beginner's Guide *By Rev. Dr. Donna Schaper and Rev. Dr. Carole Ann Camp* 6 x 9, 208 pp, b/w illus. and photos, Quality PB, 978-1-59473-486-1 **$16.99**

Lectio Divina—The Sacred Art
Transforming Words & Images into Heart-Centered Prayer
By Christine Valters Paintner, PhD 5½ x 8½, 240 pp, Quality PB, 978-1-59473-300-0 **$16.99**

Pilgrimage—The Sacred Art: Journey to the Center of the Heart
By Dr. Sheryl A. Kujawa-Holbrook 5½ x 8½, 240 pp, Quality PB, 978-1-59473-472-4 **$16.99**

Practicing the Sacred Art of Listening
A Guide to Enrich Your Relationships and Kindle Your Spiritual Life
By Kay Lindahl 8 x 8, 176 pp, Quality PB, 978-1-893361-85-0 **$18.99**

Recovery—The Sacred Art: The Twelve Steps as Spiritual Practice *By Rami Shapiro*
Foreword by Joan Borysenko, PhD 5½ x 8½, 240 pp, Quality PB, 978-1-59473-259-1 **$16.99**

Running—The Sacred Art: Preparing to Practice *By Dr. Warren A. Kay*
Foreword by Kristin Armstrong 5½ x 8½, 160 pp, Quality PB, 978-1-59473-227-0 **$16.99**

The Sacred Art of Chant: Preparing to Practice
By Ana Hernández 5½ x 8½, 192 pp, Quality PB, 978-1-59473-036-8 **$16.99**

The Sacred Art of Fasting: Preparing to Practice
By Thomas Ryan, CSP 5½ x 8½, 192 pp, Quality PB, 978-1-59473-078-8 **$15.99**

The Sacred Art of Forgiveness: Forgiving Ourselves and Others through God's Grace
By Marcia Ford 8 x 8, 176 pp, Quality PB, 978-1-59473-175-4 **$18.99**

The Sacred Art of Listening: Forty Reflections for Cultivating a Spiritual Practice
By Kay Lindahl; Illus. by Amy Schnapper 8 x 8, 160 pp, b/w illus., Quality PB, 978-1-893361-44-7 **$16.99**

The Sacred Art of Lovingkindness: Preparing to Practice
By Rabbi Rami Shapiro; Foreword by Marcia Ford 5½ x 8½, 176 pp, Quality PB, 978-1-59473-151-8 **$16.99**

Spiritual Adventures in the Snow: Skiing & Snowboarding as Renewal for Your Soul
By Dr. Marcia McFee and Rev. Karen Foster; Foreword by Paul Arthur
5½ x 8½, 208 pp, Quality PB, 978-1-59473-270-6 **$16.99**

Thanking & Blessing—The Sacred Art: Spiritual Vitality through Gratefulness
By Jay Marshall, PhD; Foreword by Philip Gulley 5½ x 8½, 176 pp, Quality PB, 978-1-59473-231-7 **$16.99**

Writing—The Sacred Art: Beyond the Page to Spiritual Practice
By Rami Shapiro and Aaron Shapiro 5½ x 8½, 192 pp, Quality PB, 978-1-59473-372-7 **$16.99**

Spirituality

Mere Spirituality
The Spiritual Life According to Henri Nouwen
By Wil Hernandez, PhD, Obl. OSB; Foreword by Ronald Rolheiser
This introduction to Nouwen's spiritual thought distills key insights on the realm of the spiritual life into one concise and compelling overview of his spirituality of the heart.
6 x 9, 160 pp, Quality PB, 978-1-59473-586-8 **$16.99**

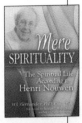

The Forgiveness Handbook
Spiritual Wisdom and Practice for the Journey to Freedom, Healing and Peace
Created by the Editors at SkyLight Paths; Introduction by The Rev. Canon Marianne Wells Borg
Offers inspiration, encouragement and spiritual practice from across faith traditions for all who seek hope, wholeness and the freedom that comes from true forgiveness.
6 x 9, 256 pp, Quality PB, 978-1-59473-577-6 **$18.99**

Like a Child
Restoring the Awe, Wonder, Joy and Resiliency of the Human Spirit
By Rev. Timothy J. Mooney
By breaking free from our misperceptions about what it means to be an adult, we can reshape our world and become harbingers of grace. This unique spiritual resource explores Jesus's counsel to become like children in order to enter the kingdom of God. 6 x 9, 160 pp, Quality PB, 978-1-59473-543-1 **$16.99**

The Passionate Jesus: What We Can Learn from Jesus about Love, Fear, Grief, Joy and Living Authentically
By The Rev. Peter Wallace
Reveals Jesus as a passionate figure who was involved, present, connected, honest and direct with others and encourages you to build personal authenticity in every area of your own life. 6 x 9, 208 pp, Quality PB, 978-1-59473-393-2 **$18.99**

Gathering at God's Table: The Meaning of Mission in the Feast of Faith
By Katharine Jefferts Schori
A profound reminder of our role in the larger frame of God's dream for a restored and reconciled world. 6 x 9, 256 pp, HC, 978-1-59473-316-1 **$21.99**

The Heartbeat of God: Finding the Sacred in the Middle of Everything
By Katharine Jefferts Schori; Foreword by Joan Chittister, OSB
Explores our connections to other people, to other nations and with the environment through the lens of faith.
6 x 9, 240 pp, HC, 978-1-59473-292-8 **$21.99**; Quality PB, 978-1-59473-589-9 **$16.99**

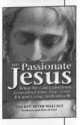

Laugh Your Way to Grace: Reclaiming the Spiritual Power of Humor
By Rev. Susan Sparks
A powerful, humorous case for laughter as a spiritual, healing path.
6 x 9, 176 pp, Quality PB, 978-1-59473-280-5 **$16.99**

Claiming Earth as Common Ground: The Ecological Crisis through the Lens of Faith
By Andrea Cohen-Kiener; Foreword by Rev. Sally Bingham
6 x 9, 192 pp, Quality PB, 978-1-59473-261-4 **$16.99**

Living into Hope: A Call to Spiritual Action for Such a Time as This
By Rev. Dr. Joan Brown Campbell; Foreword by Karen Armstrong
6 x 9, 208 pp, Quality PB, 978-1-59473-436-6 **$18.99**; HC, 978-1-59473-283-6 **$21.99**

Renewal in the Wilderness
A Spiritual Guide to Connecting with God in the Natural World
By John Lionberger 6 x 9, 176 pp, b/w photos, Quality PB, 978-1-59473-219-5 **$16.99**

A Walk with Four Spiritual Guides: Krishna, Buddha, Jesus, and Ramakrishna
By Andrew Harvey 5½ x 8½, 192 pp, b/w photos & illus., Quality PB, 978-1-59473-138-9 **$18.99**

Women's Interest

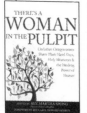

There's a Woman in the Pulpit: Christian Clergywomen Share Their Hard Days, Holy Moments & the Healing Power of Humor
Edited by Rev. Martha Spong; Foreword by Rev. Carol Howard Merritt
Offers insight into the lives of Christian clergywomen and the rigors that come with commitment to religious life, representing fourteen denominations as well as dozens of seminaries and colleges. 6 x 9, 240 pp, Quality PB, 978-1-59473-588-2 **$18.99**

She Lives! Sophia Wisdom Works in the World
By Rev. Jann Aldredge-Clanton, PhD
Fascinating narratives of clergy and laypeople who are changing the institutional church and society by restoring biblical female divine names and images to Christian theology, worship symbolism and liturgical language.
6 x 9, 320 pp, Quality PB, 978-1-59473-573-8 **$18.99**

Birthing God: Women's Experiences of the Divine
By Lana Dalberg; Foreword by Kathe Schaaf
Powerful narratives of suffering, love and hope that inspire both personal and collective transformation. 6 x 9, 304 pp, Quality PB, 978-1-59473-480-9 **$18.99**

Women, Spirituality and Transformative Leadership
Where Grace Meets Power
Edited by Kathe Schaaf, Kay Lindahl, Kathleen S. Hurty, PhD, and Reverend Guo Cheen
A dynamic conversation on the power of women's spiritual leadership and its emerging patterns of transformation.
6 x 9, 288 pp, Quality PB, 978-1-59473-548-6 **$18.99**; HC, 978-1-59473-313-0 **$24.99**

Spiritually Healthy Divorce: Navigating Disruption with Insight & Hope
By Carolyne Call A spiritual map to help you move through the twists and turns of divorce. 6 x 9, 224 pp, Quality PB, 978-1-59473-288-1 **$16.99**

Bread, Body, Spirit: Finding the Sacred in Food
Edited and with Introductions by Alice Peck 6 x 9, 224 pp, Quality PB, 978-1-59473-242-3 **$19.99**

Dance—The Sacred Art: The Joy of Movement as a Spiritual Practice
By Cynthia Winton-Henry 5½ x 8½, 224 pp, Quality PB, 978-1-59473-268-3 **$16.99**

Daughters of the Desert: Stories of Remarkable Women from Christian, Jewish and Muslim Traditions *By Claire Rudolf Murphy, Meghan Nuttall Sayres, Mary Cronk Farrell, Sarah Conover and Betsy Wharton*
5½ x 8½, 192 pp, Illus., Quality PB, 978-1-59473-106-8 **$18.99** Inc. reader's discussion guide

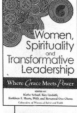

The Divine Feminine in Biblical Wisdom Literature
Selections Annotated & Explained
Translation & Annotation by Rabbi Rami Shapiro; Foreword by Rev. Cynthia Bourgeault, PhD
5½ x 8½, 240 pp, Quality PB, 978-1-59473-109-9 **$18.99**

Divining the Body: Reclaim the Holiness of Your Physical Self
By Jan Phillips 8 x 8, 256 pp, Quality PB, 978-1-59473-080-1 **$18.99**

Honoring Motherhood: Prayers, Ceremonies & Blessings
Edited and with Introductions by Lynn L. Caruso
5 x 7¼, 272 pp, Quality PB, 978-1-58473-384-0 **$9.99**; HC, 978-1-59473-239-3 **$19.99**

New Feminist Christianity: Many Voices, Many Views
Edited by Mary E. Hunt and Diann L. Neu
6 x 9, 384 pp, Quality PB, 978-1-59473-435-9 **$19.99**; HC, 978-1-59473-285-0 **$24.99**

Next to Godliness: Finding the Sacred in Housekeeping
Edited by Alice Peck 6 x 9, 224 pp, Quality PB, 978-1-59473-214-0 **$19.99**

The Triumph of Eve & Other Subversive Bible Tales
By Matt Biers-Ariel 5½ x 8½, 192 pp, Quality PB, 978-1-59473-176-1 **$14.99**

Woman Spirit Awakening in Nature: Growing into the Fullness of Who You Are
By Nancy Barrett Chickerneo, PhD; Foreword by Eileen Fisher
8 x 8, 224 pp, b/w illus., Quality PB, 978-1-59473-250-8 **$16.99**

Women of Color Pray: Voices of Strength, Faith, Healing, Hope and Courage
Edited and with Introductions by Christal M. Jackson 5 x 7¼, 208 pp, Quality PB, 978-1-59473-077-1 **$15.99**

Personal Growth

Grieving with Your Whole Heart
Spiritual Wisdom and Practice for Finding Comfort, Hope and Healing after Loss
Created by the Editors at SkyLight Paths; Introduction by Thomas Moore
A spiritual companion that embraces wisdom from across faith traditions to help
readers honor, grieve and heal from the losses they face in their lives.
6 x 9, 272 pp, Quality PB, 978-1-59473-599-8 **$18.99**

Forgiving Others, Forgiving Ourselves
Understanding & Healing Our Emotional Wounds
By Myra Warren Isenhart, PhD, and Michael Spangle, PhD
A dynamic look at forgiveness, focusing on heart, mind and soul to discover psy-
chological insights and practical steps to forgive and seek forgiveness.
6 x 9, 160 pp, Quality PB, 978-1-59473-600-1 **$16.99**

Deepening Engagement
Essential Wisdom for Listening and Leading with Purpose, Meaning and Joy
By Diane M. Millis, PhD; Foreword by Rob Lehman
A toolkit for community building as well as a resource for personal growth and
small group enrichment.
5 x 7¼, 176 pp, Quality PB, 978-1-59473-584-4 **$14.99**

The Forgiveness Handbook
Spiritual Wisdom and Practice for the Journey to Freedom, Healing and Peace
Created by the Editors at SkyLight Paths; Introduction by The Rev. Canon Marianne Wells Borg
Offers inspiration, encouragement and spiritual practice from across faith tradi-
tions for all who seek hope, wholeness and the freedom that comes from true
forgiveness. 6 x 9, 256 pp, Quality PB, 978-1-59473-577-6 **$18.99**

Decision Making & Spiritual Discernment
The Sacred Art of Finding Your Way
By Nancy L. Bieber
Presents three essential aspects of Spirit-led decision making: willingness, atten-
tiveness and responsiveness.
5½ x 8½, 208 pp, Quality PB, 978-1-59473-289-8 **$16.99**

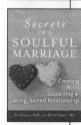

Like a Child
Restoring the Awe, Wonder, Joy and Resiliency of the Human Spirit
By Rev. Timothy J. Mooney
Explores Jesus's counsel to become like children in order to enter the kingdom of
God. 6 x 9, 160 pp, Quality PB, 978-1-59473-543-1 **$16.99**

Conversation—The Sacred Art
Practicing Presence in an Age of Distraction
By Diane M. Millis, PhD; Foreword by Rev. Tilden Edwards, PhD
5½ x 8½, 192 pp, Quality PB, 978-1-59473-474-8 **$16.99**

Hospitality—The Sacred Art
Discovering the Hidden Spiritual Power of Invitation and Welcome
By Rev. Nanette Sawyer; Foreword by Rev. Dirk Ficca
5½ x 8½, 208 pp, Quality PB, 978-1-59473-228-7 **$16.99**

The Losses of Our Lives
The Sacred Gifts of Renewal in Everyday Loss
By Dr. Nancy Copeland-Payton
6 x 9, 192 pp, Quality PB, 978-1-59473-307-9 **$16.99**; HC, 978-1-59473-271-3 **$19.99**

Secrets of a Soulful Marriage
Creating & Sustaining a Loving, Sacred Relationship
By Jim Sharon, EdD, and Ruth Sharon, MS 6 x 9, 192 pp, Quality PB, 978-1-59473-554-7 **$16.99**

A Spirituality for Brokenness
Discovering Your Deepest Self in Difficult Times
By Terry Taylor 6 x 9, 176 pp, Quality PB, 978-1-59473-229-4 **$16.99**